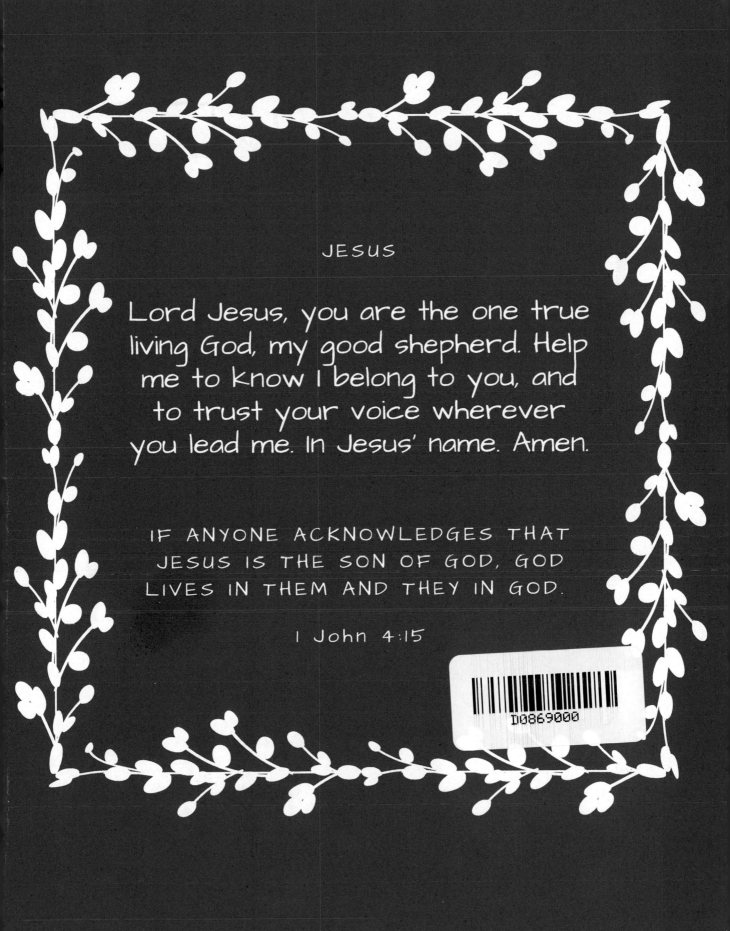

JESUS

Lord Jesus, you are the one true living God, my good shepherd. Help me to know I belong to you, and to trust your voice wherever you lead me. In Jesus' name. Amen.

IF ANYONE ACKNOWLEDGES THAT JESUS IS THE SON OF GOD, GOD LIVES IN THEM AND THEY IN GOD.

1 John 4:15

Today's verse

Date

Lord teach me

Lord guide me

Today I pray for

Prayers for others

Answered prayers

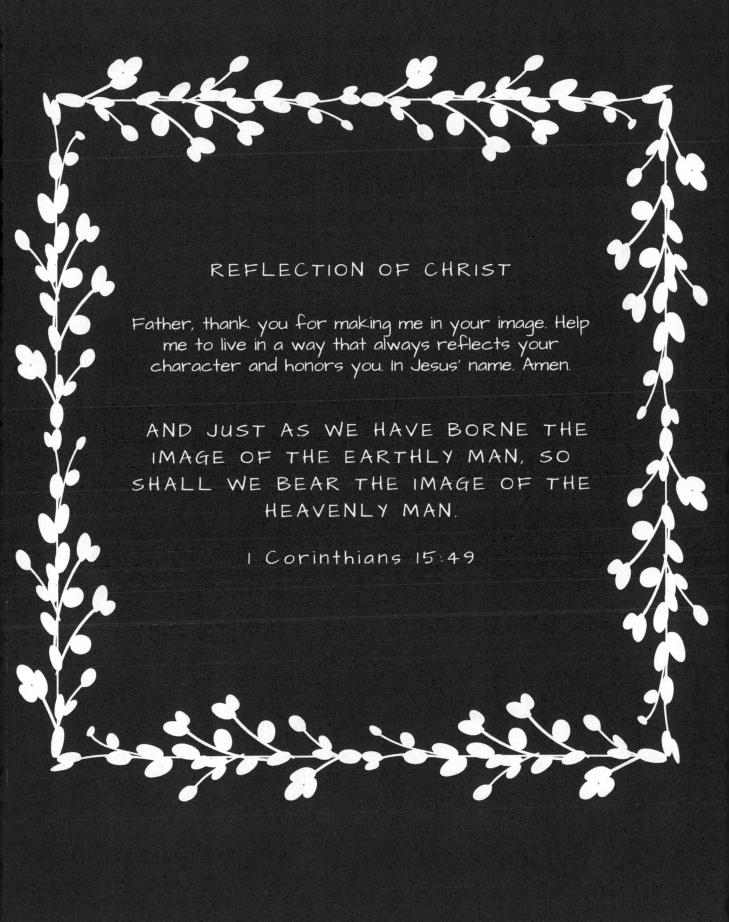

REFLECTION OF CHRIST

Father, thank you for making me in your image. Help me to live in a way that always reflects your character and honors you. In Jesus' name. Amen.

AND JUST AS WE HAVE BORNE THE IMAGE OF THE EARTHLY MAN, SO SHALL WE BEAR THE IMAGE OF THE HEAVENLY MAN.

1 Corinthians 15:49

Today's verse

Date

Lord teach me

Lord guide me

Today I pray for

Prayers for others

Answered prayers

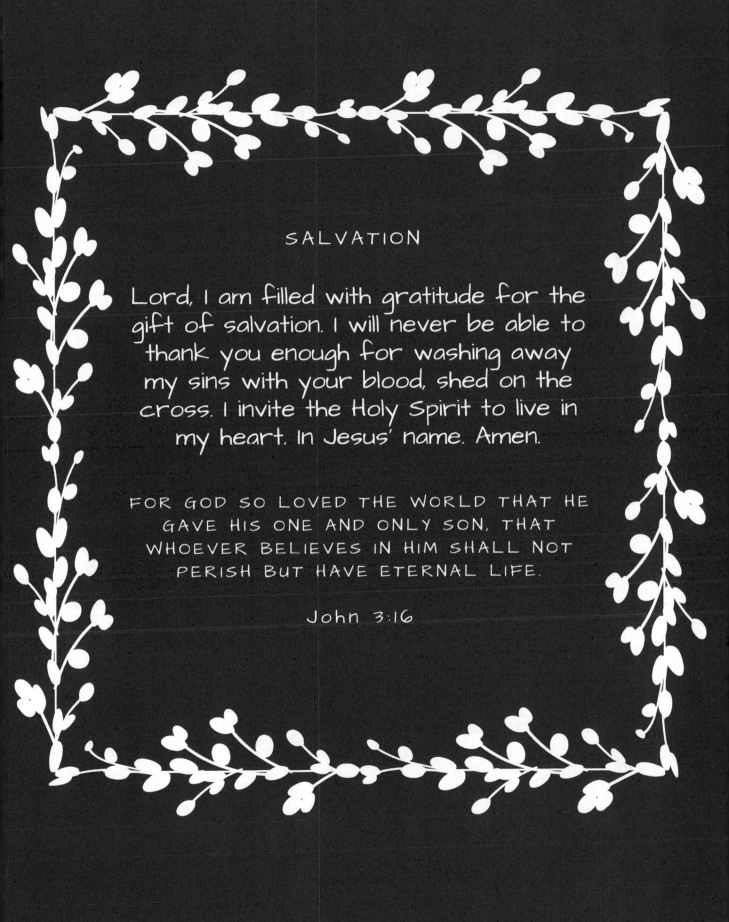

SALVATION

Lord, I am filled with gratitude for the gift of salvation. I will never be able to thank you enough for washing away my sins with your blood, shed on the cross. I invite the Holy Spirit to live in my heart. In Jesus' name. Amen.

FOR GOD SO LOVED THE WORLD THAT HE GAVE HIS ONE AND ONLY SON, THAT WHOEVER BELIEVES IN HIM SHALL NOT PERISH BUT HAVE ETERNAL LIFE.

John 3:16

Today's verse

Date

Lord teach me

Lord guide me

Today I pray for

Prayers for others

Answered prayers

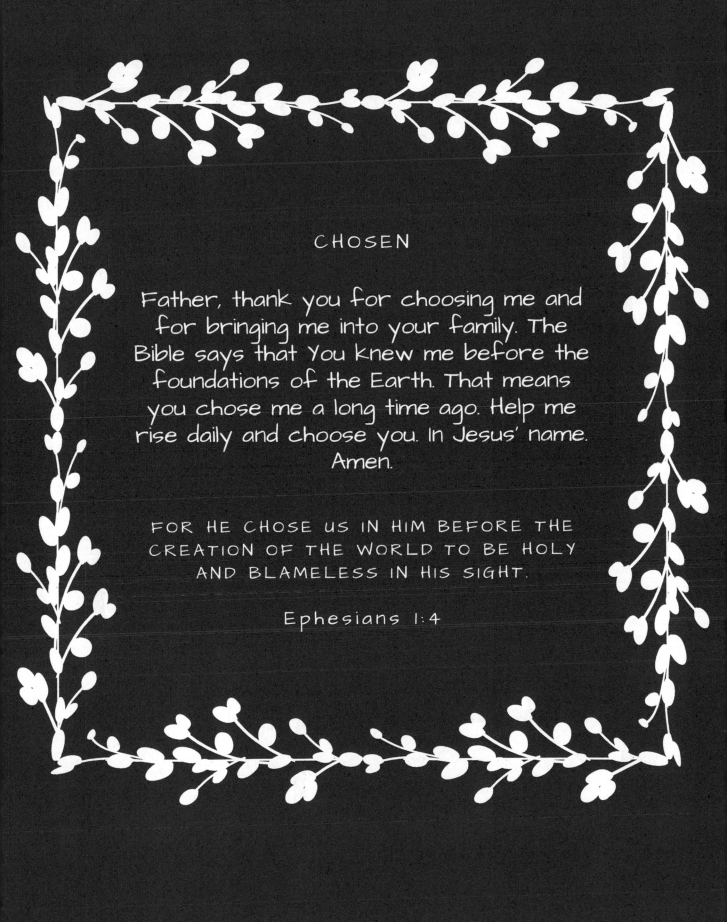

CHOSEN

Father, thank you for choosing me and for bringing me into your family. The Bible says that You knew me before the foundations of the Earth. That means you chose me a long time ago. Help me rise daily and choose you. In Jesus' name. Amen.

FOR HE CHOSE US IN HIM BEFORE THE CREATION OF THE WORLD TO BE HOLY AND BLAMELESS IN HIS SIGHT.

Ephesians 1:4

Today's verse

Date

Lord teach me

Lord guide me

Today I pray for

Prayers for others

Answered prayers

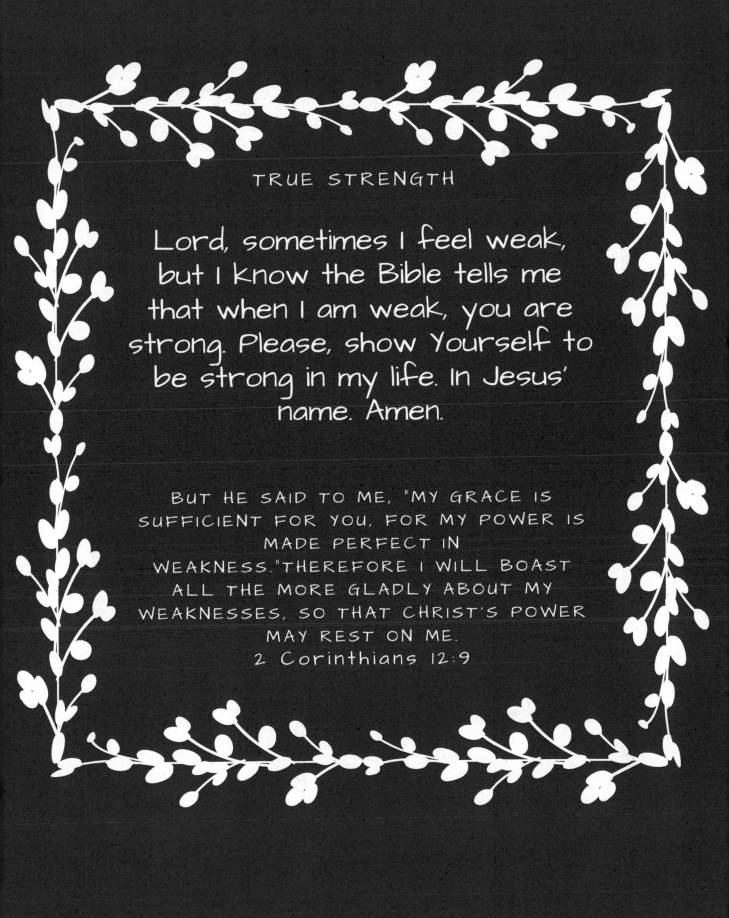

TRUE STRENGTH

Lord, sometimes I feel weak, but I know the Bible tells me that when I am weak, you are strong. Please, show Yourself to be strong in my life. In Jesus' name. Amen.

BUT HE SAID TO ME, "MY GRACE IS SUFFICIENT FOR YOU, FOR MY POWER IS MADE PERFECT IN WEAKNESS."THEREFORE I WILL BOAST ALL THE MORE GLADLY ABOUT MY WEAKNESSES, SO THAT CHRIST'S POWER MAY REST ON ME.
2 Corinthians 12:9

Today's verse

Date

Lord teach me

Lord guide me

Today I pray for

Prayers for others

Answered prayers

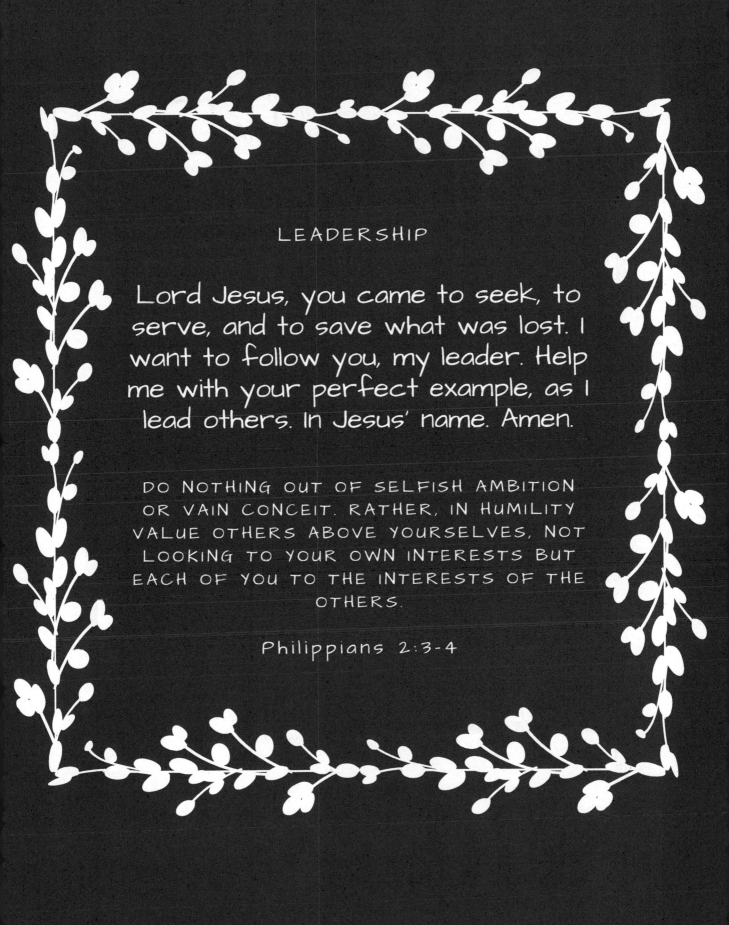

LEADERSHIP

Lord Jesus, you came to seek, to serve, and to save what was lost. I want to follow you, my leader. Help me with your perfect example, as I lead others. In Jesus' name. Amen.

DO NOTHING OUT OF SELFISH AMBITION OR VAIN CONCEIT. RATHER, IN HUMILITY VALUE OTHERS ABOVE YOURSELVES, NOT LOOKING TO YOUR OWN INTERESTS BUT EACH OF YOU TO THE INTERESTS OF THE OTHERS.

Philippians 2:3-4

Today's verse

Date

Lord teach me

Lord guide me

Today I pray for

Prayers for others

Answered prayers

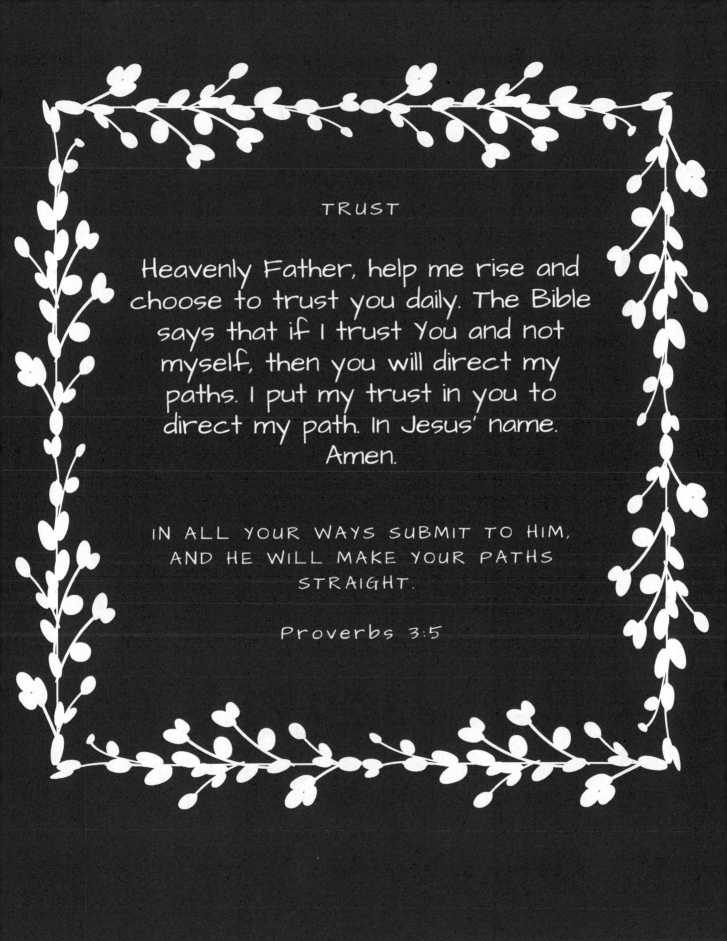

TRUST

Heavenly Father, help me rise and choose to trust you daily. The Bible says that if I trust You and not myself, then you will direct my paths. I put my trust in you to direct my path. In Jesus' name. Amen.

IN ALL YOUR WAYS SUBMIT TO HIM, AND HE WILL MAKE YOUR PATHS STRAIGHT.

Proverbs 3:5

Today's verse

Date

Lord teach me

Lord guide me

Today I pray for

Prayers for others

Answered prayers

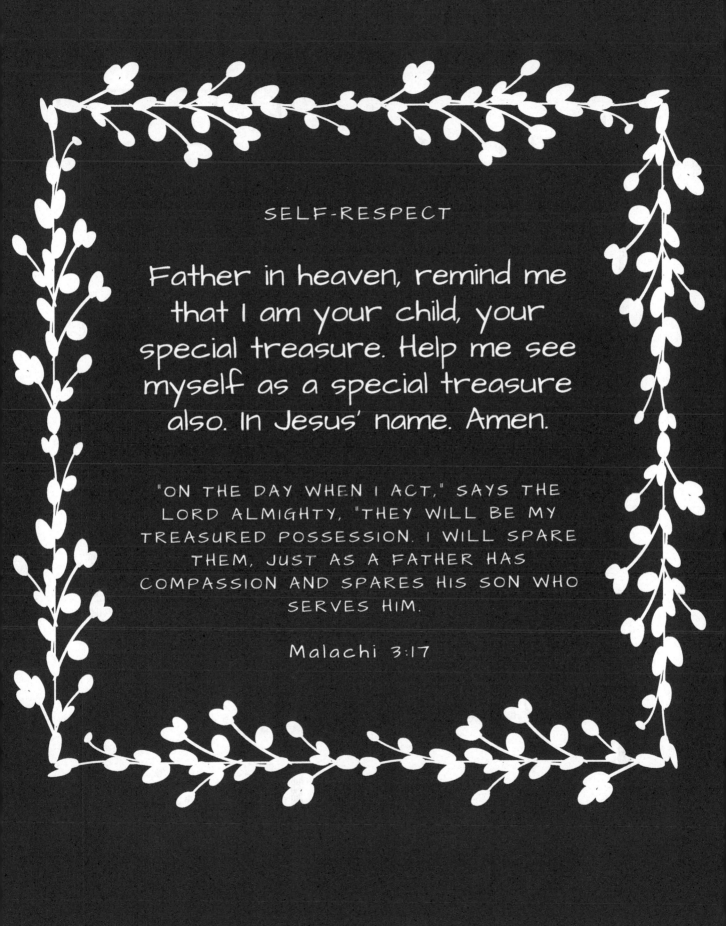

SELF-RESPECT

Father in heaven, remind me that I am your child, your special treasure. Help me see myself as a special treasure also. In Jesus' name. Amen.

"ON THE DAY WHEN I ACT," SAYS THE LORD ALMIGHTY, "THEY WILL BE MY TREASURED POSSESSION. I WILL SPARE THEM, JUST AS A FATHER HAS COMPASSION AND SPARES HIS SON WHO SERVES HIM.

Malachi 3:17

Today's verse

Date

Lord teach me

Lord guide me

Today I pray for

Prayers for others

Answered prayers

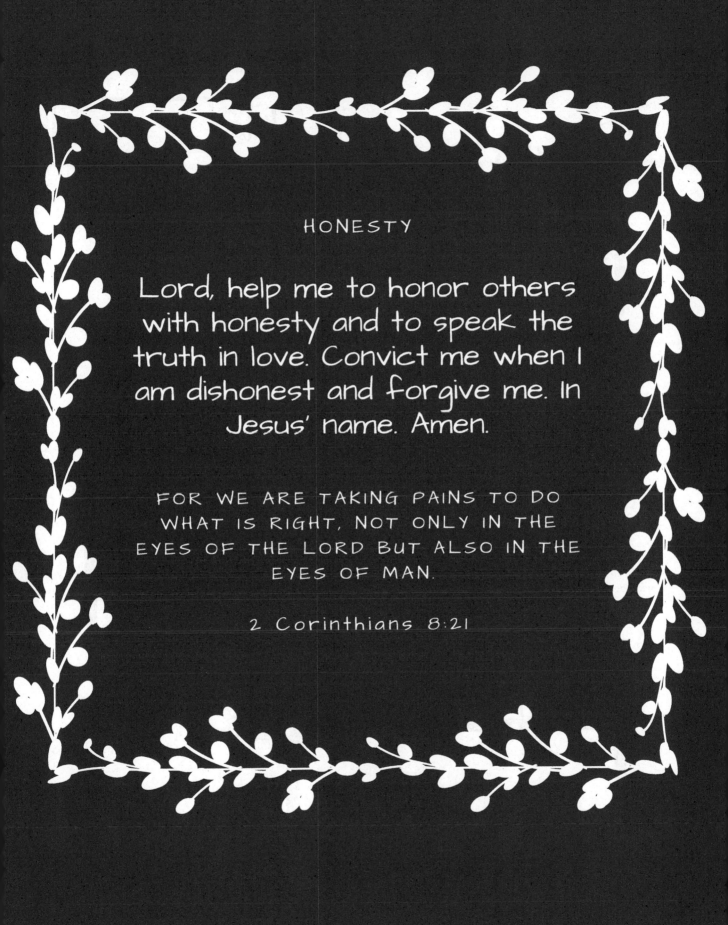

HONESTY

Lord, help me to honor others with honesty and to speak the truth in love. Convict me when I am dishonest and forgive me. In Jesus' name. Amen.

FOR WE ARE TAKING PAINS TO DO WHAT IS RIGHT, NOT ONLY IN THE EYES OF THE LORD BUT ALSO IN THE EYES OF MAN.

2 Corinthians 8:21

Today's verse

Date

Lord teach me

Lord guide me

Today I pray for

Prayers for others

Answered prayers

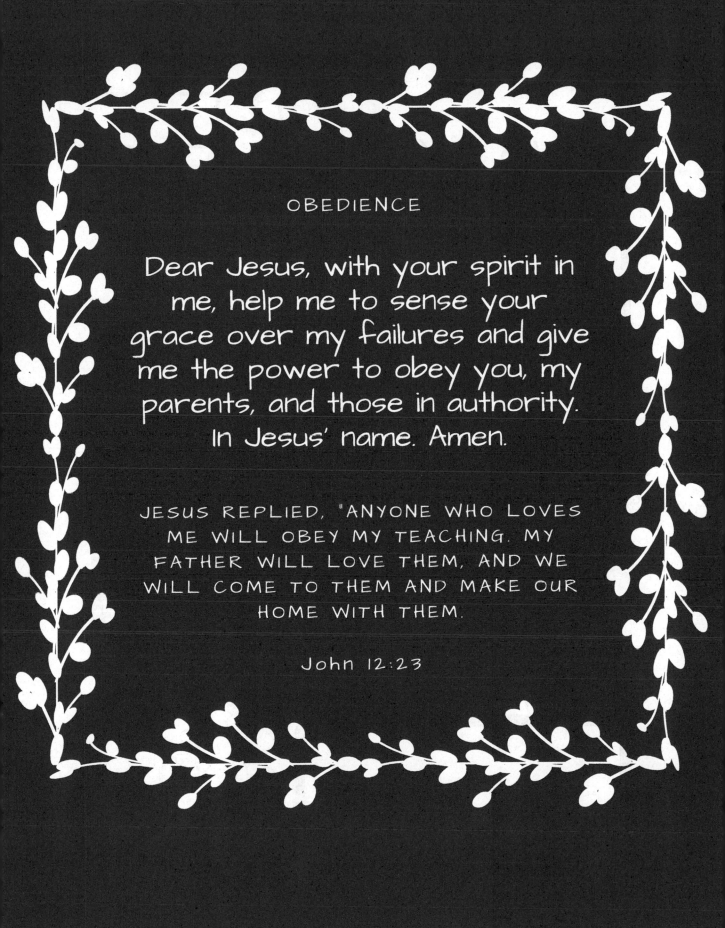

OBEDIENCE

Dear Jesus, with your spirit in me, help me to sense your grace over my failures and give me the power to obey you, my parents, and those in authority. In Jesus' name. Amen.

JESUS REPLIED, "ANYONE WHO LOVES ME WILL OBEY MY TEACHING. MY FATHER WILL LOVE THEM, AND WE WILL COME TO THEM AND MAKE OUR HOME WITH THEM.

John 12:23

Today's verse

Date

Lord teach me

Lord guide me

Today I pray for

Prayers for others

Answered prayers

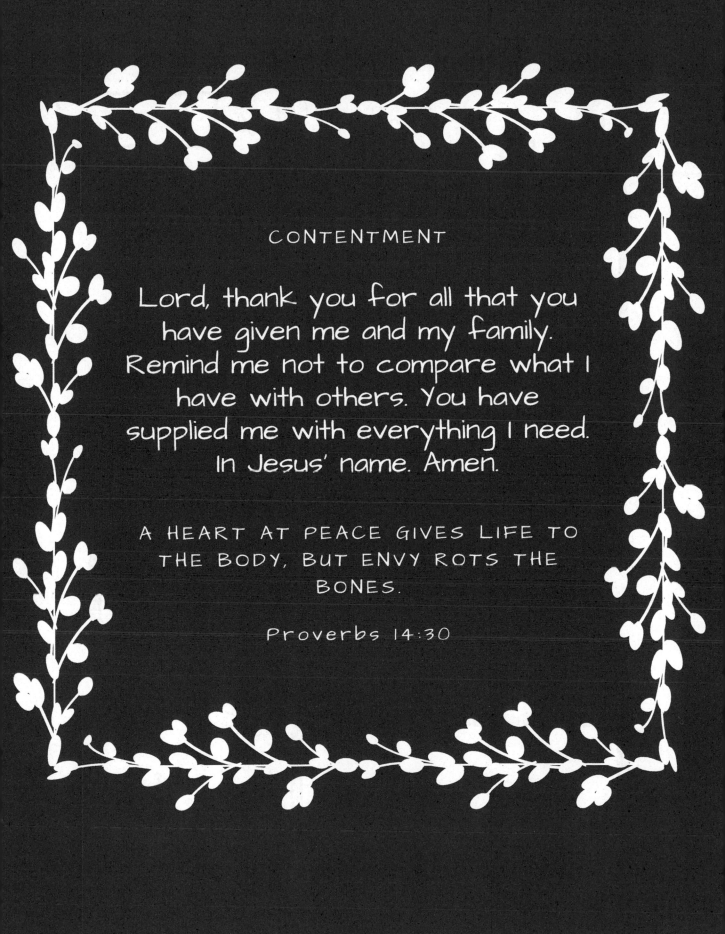

CONTENTMENT

Lord, thank you for all that you
have given me and my family.
Remind me not to compare what I
have with others. You have
supplied me with everything I need.
In Jesus' name. Amen.

A HEART AT PEACE GIVES LIFE TO
THE BODY, BUT ENVY ROTS THE
BONES.

Proverbs 14:30

Today's verse

Date

Lord teach me

Lord guide me

Today I pray for

Prayers for others

Answered prayers

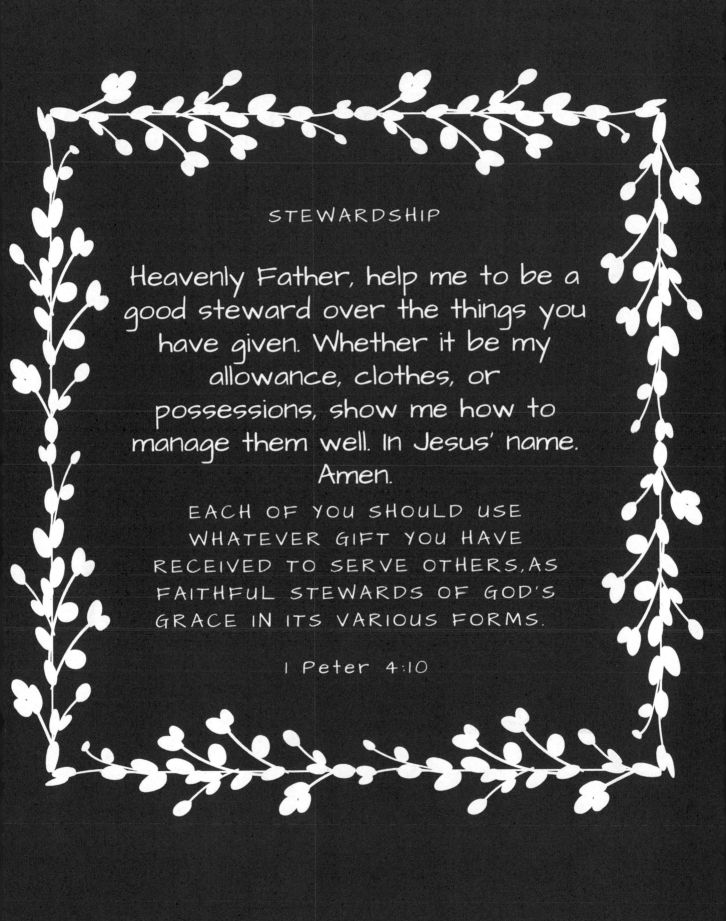

STEWARDSHIP

Heavenly Father, help me to be a good steward over the things you have given. Whether it be my allowance, clothes, or possessions, show me how to manage them well. In Jesus' name. Amen.

EACH OF YOU SHOULD USE WHATEVER GIFT YOU HAVE RECEIVED TO SERVE OTHERS, AS FAITHFUL STEWARDS OF GOD'S GRACE IN ITS VARIOUS FORMS.

1 Peter 4:10

Today's verse

Date

Lord
teach me

Lord guide me

Today I pray for

Prayers for others

Answered prayers

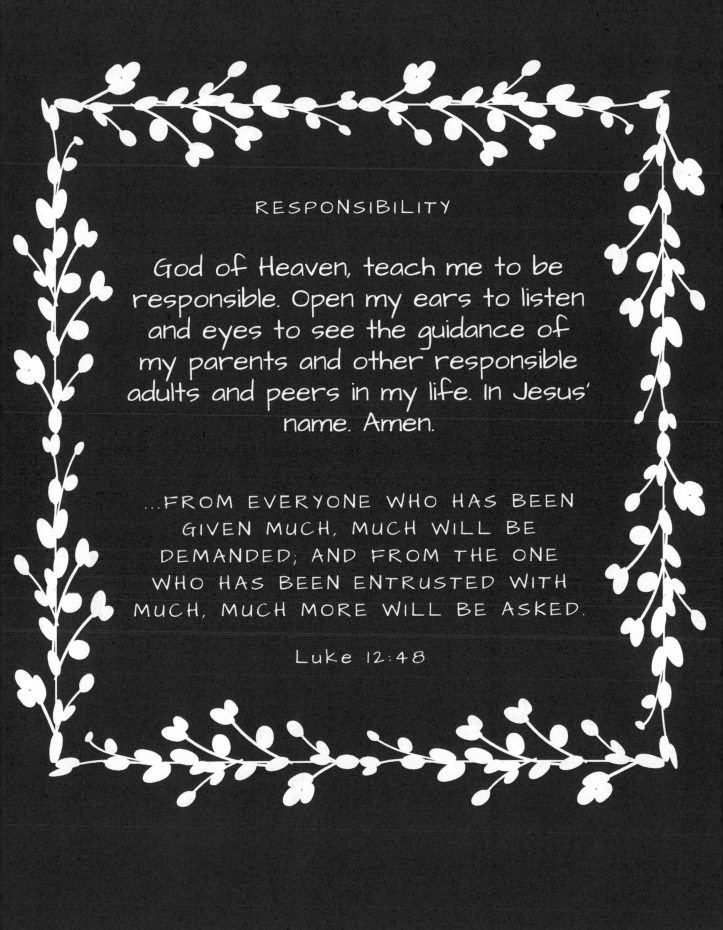

RESPONSIBILITY

God of Heaven, teach me to be
responsible. Open my ears to listen
and eyes to see the guidance of
my parents and other responsible
adults and peers in my life. In Jesus'
name. Amen.

...FROM EVERYONE WHO HAS BEEN
GIVEN MUCH, MUCH WILL BE
DEMANDED; AND FROM THE ONE
WHO HAS BEEN ENTRUSTED WITH
MUCH, MUCH MORE WILL BE ASKED.

Luke 12:48

Today's verse

Date

Lord teach me

Lord guide me

Today I pray for

Prayers for others

Answered prayers

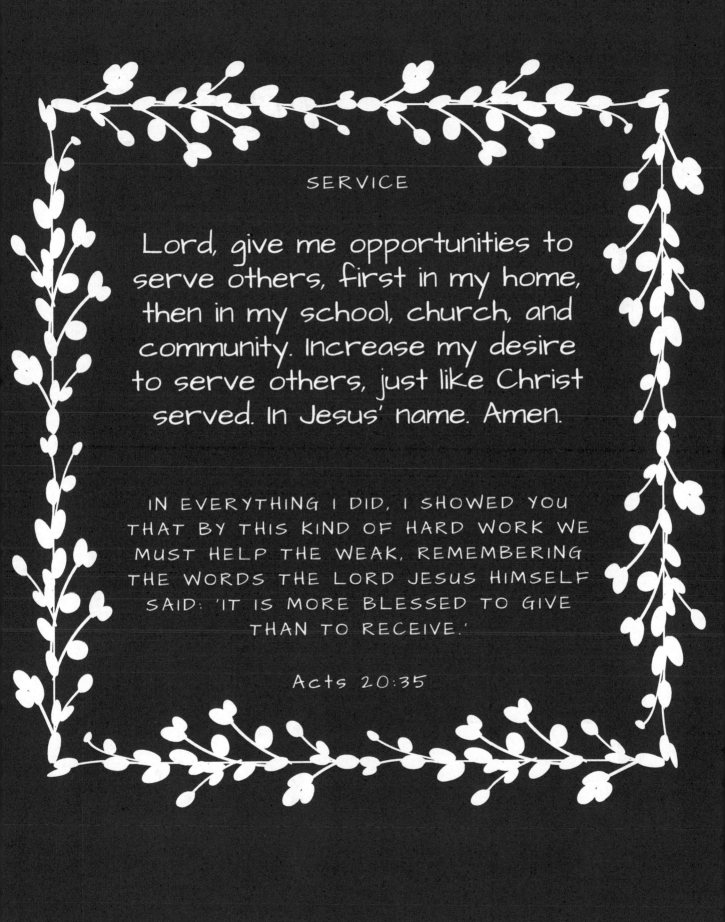

SERVICE

Lord, give me opportunities to serve others, first in my home, then in my school, church, and community. Increase my desire to serve others, just like Christ served. In Jesus' name. Amen.

IN EVERYTHING I DID, I SHOWED YOU THAT BY THIS KIND OF HARD WORK WE MUST HELP THE WEAK, REMEMBERING THE WORDS THE LORD JESUS HIMSELF SAID: 'IT IS MORE BLESSED TO GIVE THAN TO RECEIVE.'

Acts 20:35

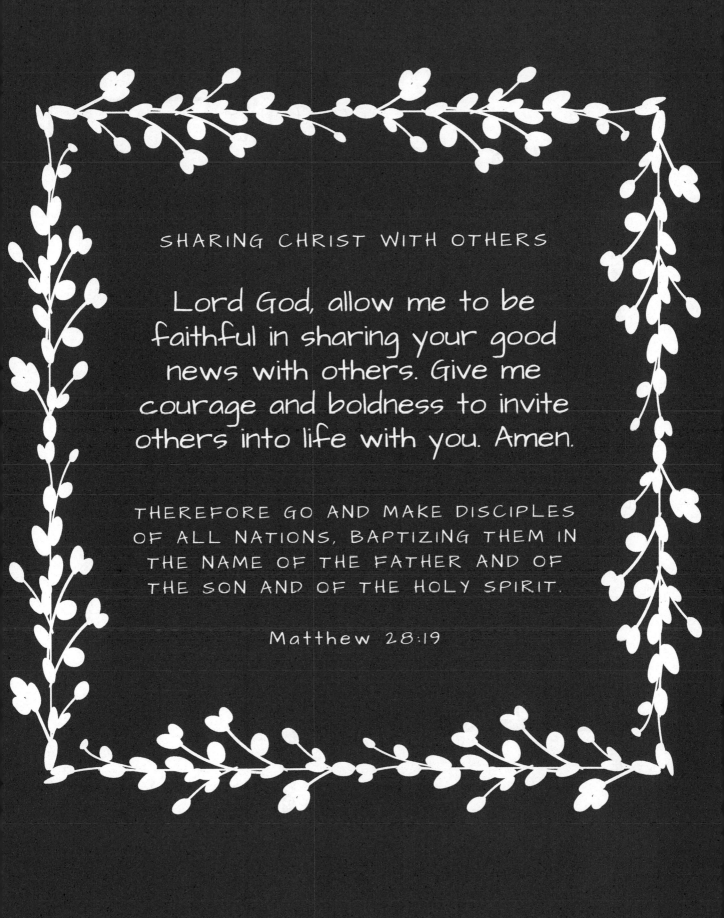

SHARING CHRIST WITH OTHERS

Lord God, allow me to be faithful in sharing your good news with others. Give me courage and boldness to invite others into life with you. Amen.

THEREFORE GO AND MAKE DISCIPLES OF ALL NATIONS, BAPTIZING THEM IN THE NAME OF THE FATHER AND OF THE SON AND OF THE HOLY SPIRIT.

Matthew 28:19

Today's verse

Date

Lord teach me

Lord guide me

Today I pray for

Prayers for others

Answered prayers

PEER PRESSURE

Heavenly Father, help me to
resist the negative influences of
my peers. Remind me to flee sin
and all things that are displeasing
to you. In Jesus' name. Amen.

MY SON, IF SINFUL MEN ENTICE YOU,
DO NOT GIVE IN TO THEM.

Proverbs 1:10

Today's verse

Date

Lord teach me

Lord guide me

Today I pray for

Prayers for others

Answered prayers

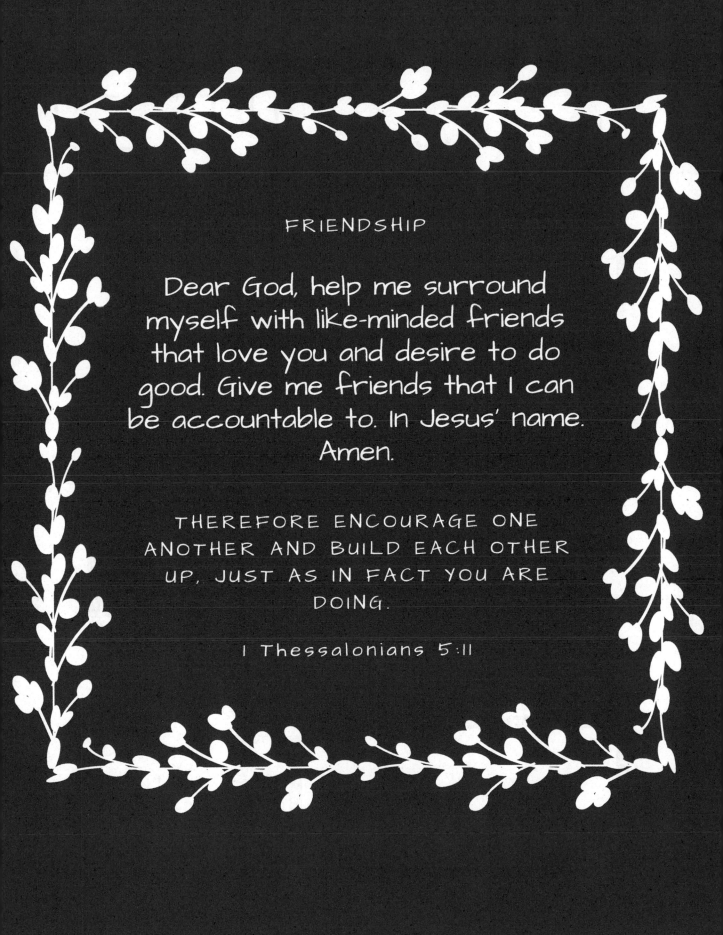

FRIENDSHIP

Dear God, help me surround myself with like-minded friends that love you and desire to do good. Give me friends that I can be accountable to. In Jesus' name. Amen.

THEREFORE ENCOURAGE ONE ANOTHER AND BUILD EACH OTHER UP, JUST AS IN FACT YOU ARE DOING.

1 Thessalonians 5:11

Today's verse

Date

Lord teach me

Lord guide me

Today I pray for

Prayers for others

Answered prayers

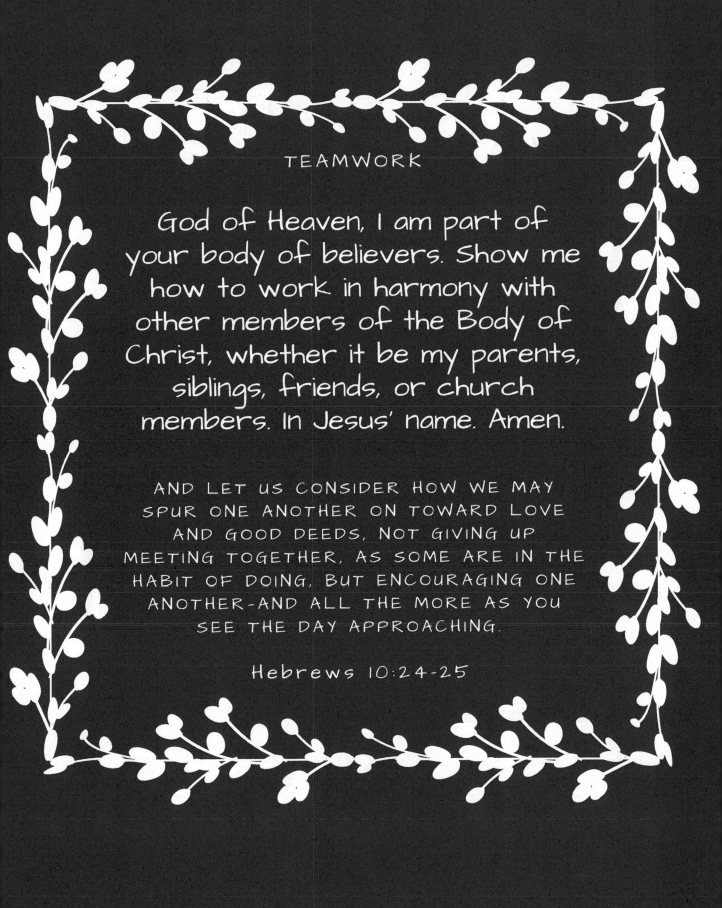

TEAMWORK

God of Heaven, I am part of your body of believers. Show me how to work in harmony with other members of the Body of Christ, whether it be my parents, siblings, friends, or church members. In Jesus' name. Amen.

AND LET US CONSIDER HOW WE MAY SPUR ONE ANOTHER ON TOWARD LOVE AND GOOD DEEDS, NOT GIVING UP MEETING TOGETHER, AS SOME ARE IN THE HABIT OF DOING, BUT ENCOURAGING ONE ANOTHER-AND ALL THE MORE AS YOU SEE THE DAY APPROACHING.

Hebrews 10:24-25

Today's verse

Date

Lord teach me

Lord guide me

Today I pray for

Prayers for others

Answered prayers

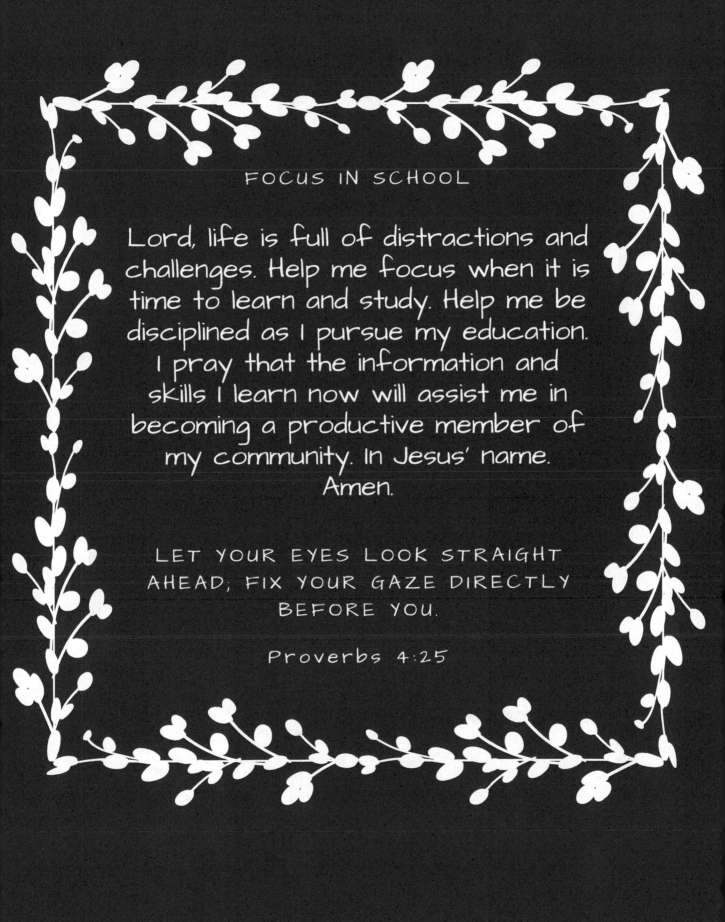

FOCUS IN SCHOOL

Lord, life is full of distractions and challenges. Help me focus when it is time to learn and study. Help me be disciplined as I pursue my education. I pray that the information and skills I learn now will assist me in becoming a productive member of my community. In Jesus' name. Amen.

LET YOUR EYES LOOK STRAIGHT AHEAD; FIX YOUR GAZE DIRECTLY BEFORE YOU.

Proverbs 4:25

Today's verse

Date

Lord teach me

Lord guide me

Today I pray for

Prayers for others

Answered prayers

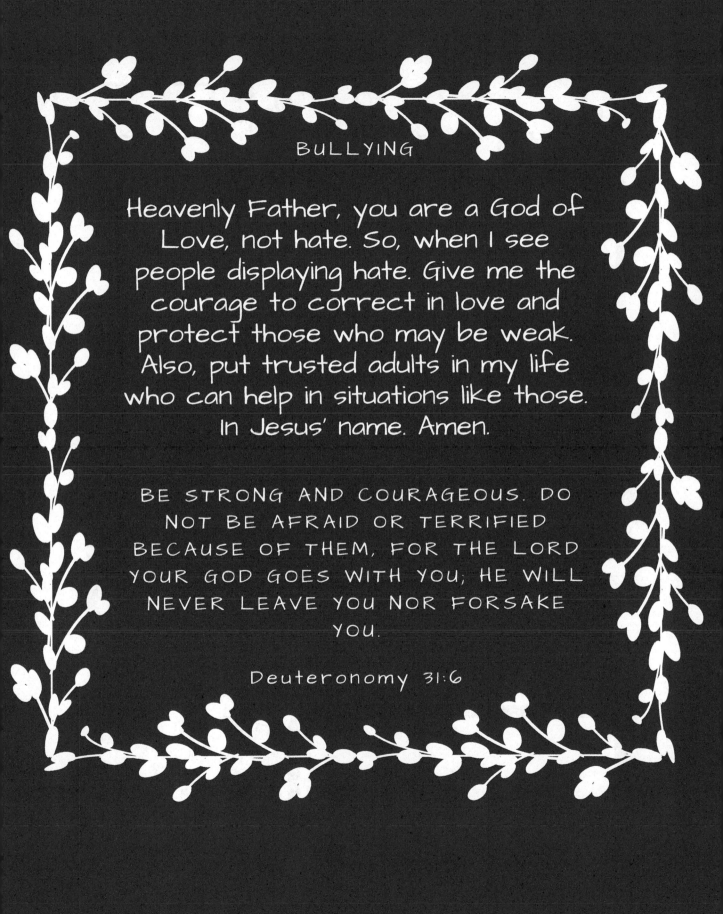

BULLYING

Heavenly Father, you are a God of Love, not hate. So, when I see people displaying hate. Give me the courage to correct in love and protect those who may be weak. Also, put trusted adults in my life who can help in situations like those. In Jesus' name. Amen.

BE STRONG AND COURAGEOUS. DO NOT BE AFRAID OR TERRIFIED BECAUSE OF THEM, FOR THE LORD YOUR GOD GOES WITH YOU; HE WILL NEVER LEAVE YOU NOR FORSAKE YOU.

Deuteronomy 31:6

Today's verse

Date

Lord teach me

Lord guide me

Today I pray for

Prayers for others

Answered prayers

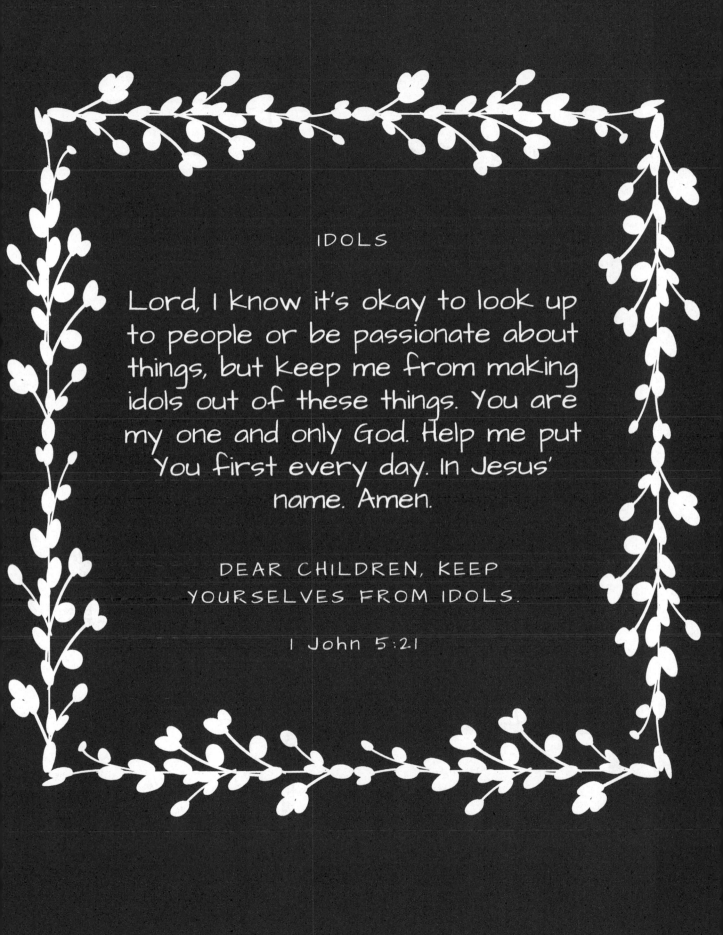

IDOLS

Lord, I know it's okay to look up to people or be passionate about things, but keep me from making idols out of these things. You are my one and only God. Help me put You first every day. In Jesus' name. Amen.

DEAR CHILDREN, KEEP YOURSELVES FROM IDOLS.

1 John 5:21

Today's verse

Date

Lord teach me

Lord guide me

Today I pray for

Prayers for others

Answered prayers

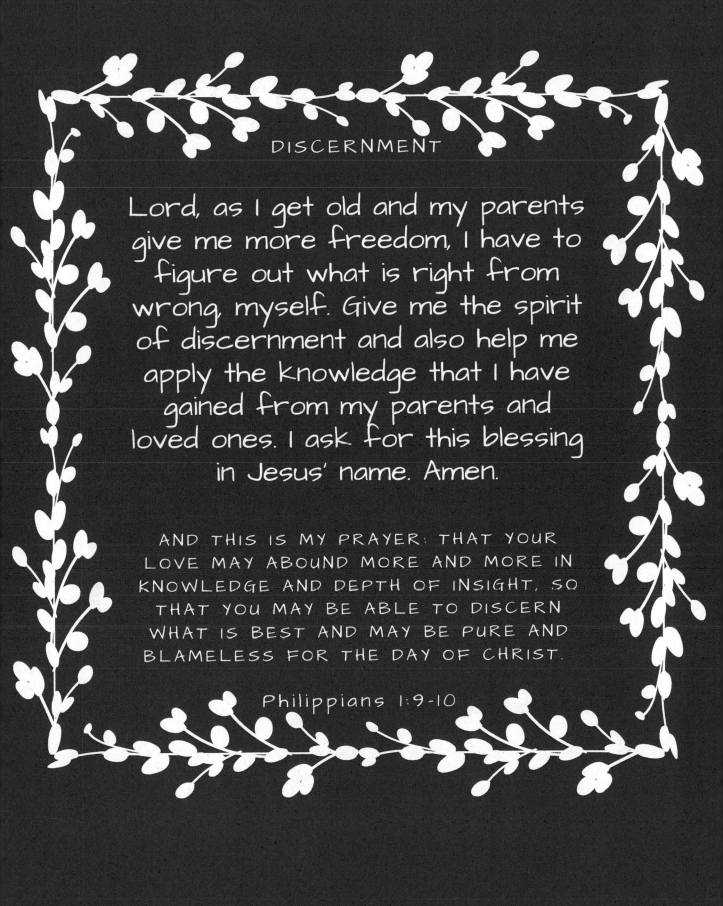

DISCERNMENT

Lord, as I get old and my parents give me more freedom, I have to figure out what is right from wrong, myself. Give me the spirit of discernment and also help me apply the knowledge that I have gained from my parents and loved ones. I ask for this blessing in Jesus' name. Amen.

AND THIS IS MY PRAYER: THAT YOUR LOVE MAY ABOUND MORE AND MORE IN KNOWLEDGE AND DEPTH OF INSIGHT, SO THAT YOU MAY BE ABLE TO DISCERN WHAT IS BEST AND MAY BE PURE AND BLAMELESS FOR THE DAY OF CHRIST.

Philippians 1:9-10

Today's verse

Date

Lord teach me

Lord guide me

Today I pray for

Prayers
for others

Answered prayers

PURITY

Dear Lord, remind me that my body and mind belong to You. Help me be mindful of what I put into Your body and mind. I want to put in things that are pleasing to You. In Jesus' name. Amen.

FINALLY, BROTHERS AND SISTERS, WHATEVER IS TRUE, WHATEVER IS NOBLE, WHATEVER IS RIGHT, WHATEVER IS PURE, WHATEVER IS LOVELY, WHATEVER IS ADMIRABLE-IF ANYTHING IS EXCELLENT OR PRAISEWORTHY-THINK ABOUT SUCH THINGS.

Philippians 4:8

Today's verse

Date

Lord teach me

Lord guide me

Today I pray for

Prayers for others

Answered prayers

SOCIAL MEDIA

Heavenly Father, while social media is fun and entertaining. Help me guard my eyes, ears, and heart. Help me be mindful of what I take in. In Jesus' name. Amen.

I HAVE THE RIGHT TO DO ANYTHING," YOU SAY-BUT NOT EVERYTHING IS BENEFICIAL. "I HAVE THE RIGHT TO DO ANYTHING"-BUT NOT EVERYTHING IS CONSTRUCTIVE.

1 Corinthians 10:23

Today's verse

Date

Lord
teach me

Lord guide me

Today I pray for

Prayers for others

Answered prayers

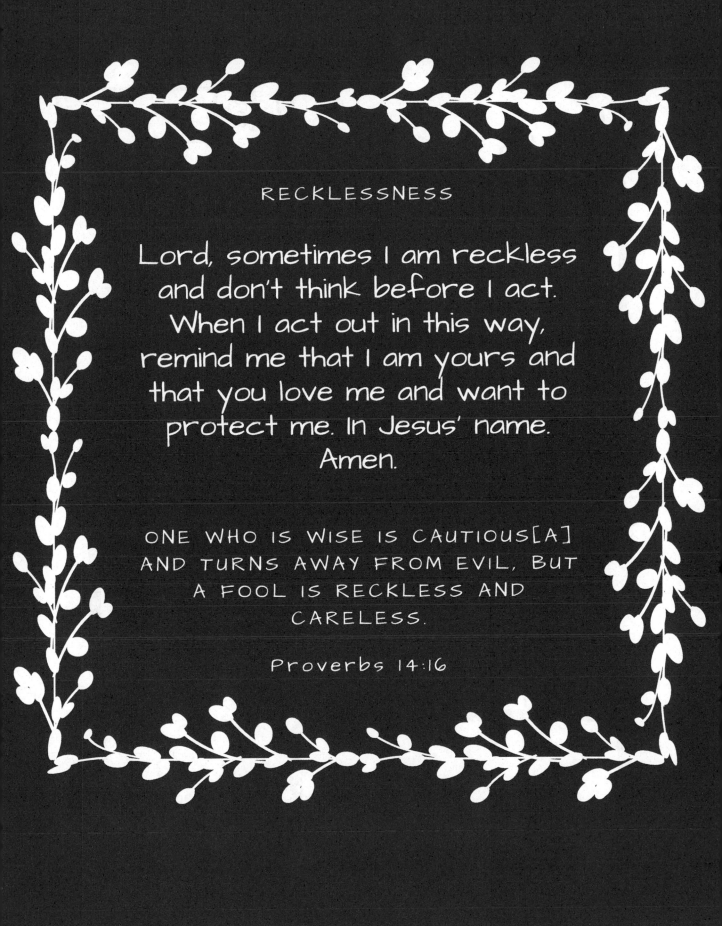

RECKLESSNESS

Lord, sometimes I am reckless
and don't think before I act.
When I act out in this way,
remind me that I am yours and
that you love me and want to
protect me. In Jesus' name.
Amen.

ONE WHO IS WISE IS CAUTIOUS[A]
AND TURNS AWAY FROM EVIL, BUT
A FOOL IS RECKLESS AND
CARELESS.

Proverbs 14:16

Today's verse

Date

Lord teach me

Lord guide me

Today I pray for

Prayers for others

Answered prayers

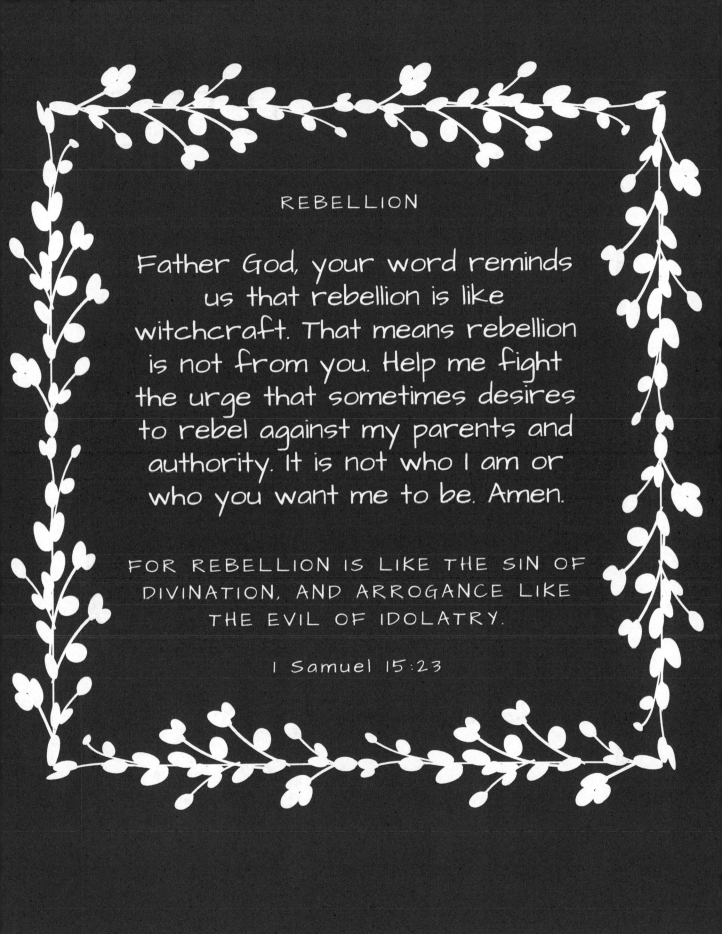

REBELLION

Father God, your word reminds us that rebellion is like witchcraft. That means rebellion is not from you. Help me fight the urge that sometimes desires to rebel against my parents and authority. It is not who I am or who you want me to be. Amen.

FOR REBELLION IS LIKE THE SIN OF DIVINATION, AND ARROGANCE LIKE THE EVIL OF IDOLATRY.

1 Samuel 15:23

Today's verse

Date

Lord teach me

Lord guide me

Today I pray for

Prayers for others

Answered prayers

PRIDE

Lord of Heaven, whenever I get too proud, remind me that pride is just another form of sin. I want to glorify you with all that I do. In Jesus' name. Amen.

WHEN PRIDE COMES, THEN COMES DISGRACE, BUT WITH HUMILITY COMES WISDOM.

Proverbs 11:2

Today's verse

Date

Lord teach me

Lord guide me

Today I pray for

Prayers for others

Answered prayers

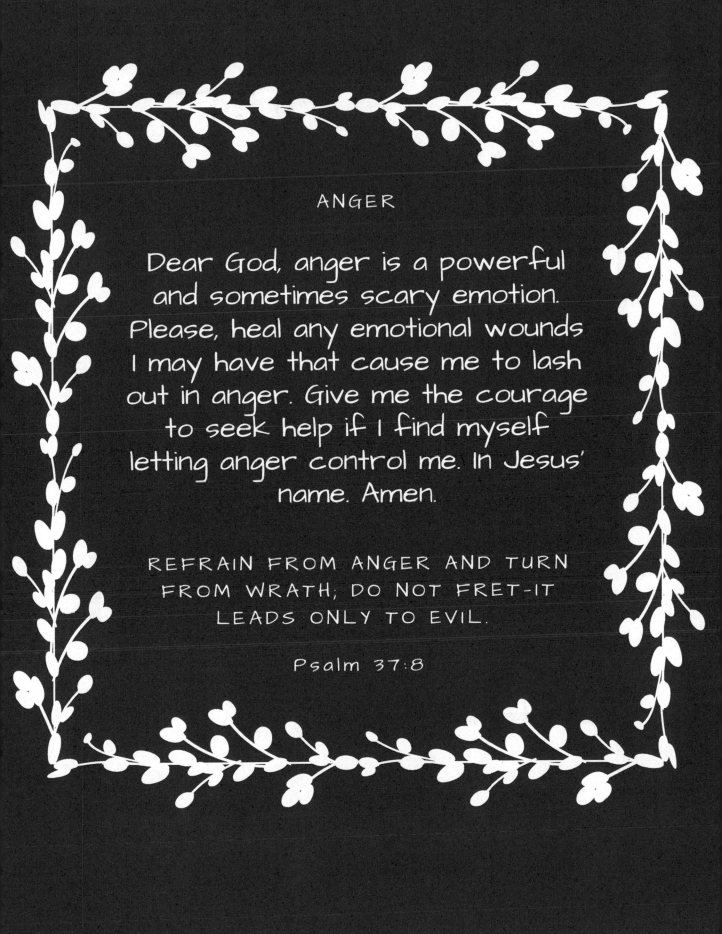

ANGER

Dear God, anger is a powerful
and sometimes scary emotion.
Please, heal any emotional wounds
I may have that cause me to lash
out in anger. Give me the courage
to seek help if I find myself
letting anger control me. In Jesus'
name. Amen.

REFRAIN FROM ANGER AND TURN
FROM WRATH; DO NOT FRET-IT
LEADS ONLY TO EVIL.

Psalm 37:8

Today's verse

Date

Lord teach me

Lord guide me

Today I pray for

Prayers for others

Answered prayers

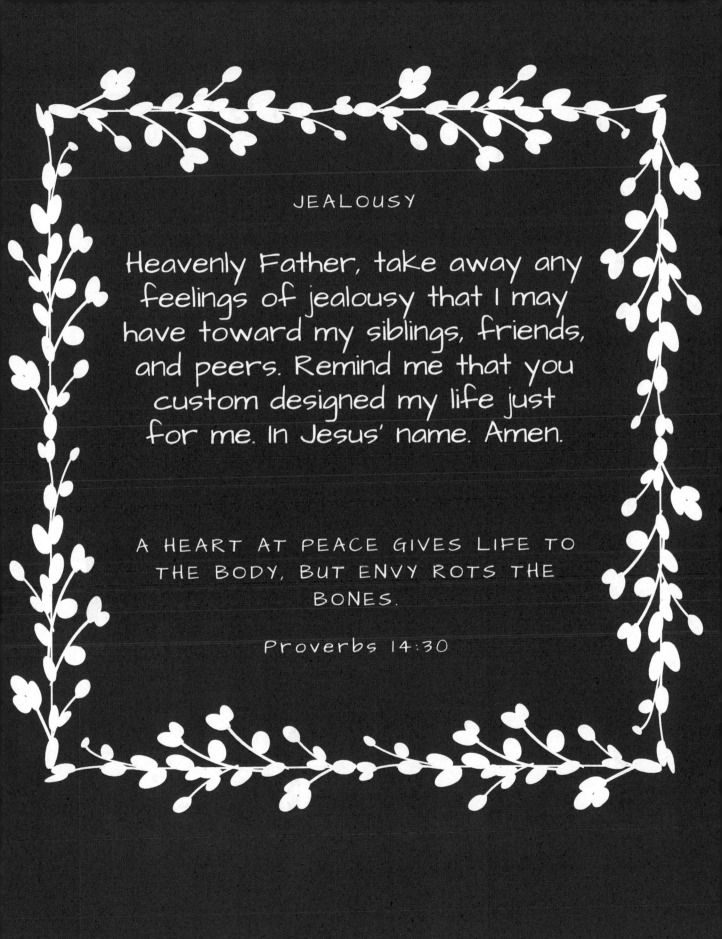

JEALOUSY

Heavenly Father, take away any feelings of jealousy that I may have toward my siblings, friends, and peers. Remind me that you custom designed my life just for me. In Jesus' name. Amen.

A HEART AT PEACE GIVES LIFE TO THE BODY, BUT ENVY ROTS THE BONES.

Proverbs 14:30

Today's verse

Date

Lord teach me

Lord guide me

Today I pray for

Prayers for others

Answered prayers

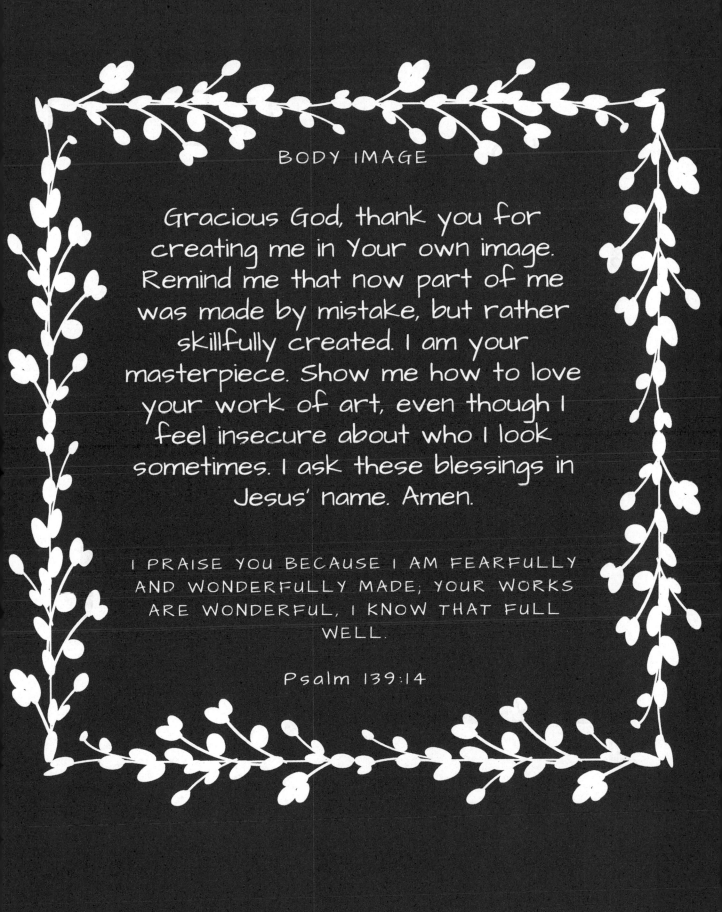

BODY IMAGE

Gracious God, thank you for creating me in Your own image. Remind me that now part of me was made by mistake, but rather skillfully created. I am your masterpiece. Show me how to love your work of art, even though I feel insecure about who I look sometimes. I ask these blessings in Jesus' name. Amen.

I PRAISE YOU BECAUSE I AM FEARFULLY AND WONDERFULLY MADE; YOUR WORKS ARE WONDERFUL, I KNOW THAT FULL WELL.

Psalm 139:14

Today's verse

Date

Lord teach me

Lord guide me

Today I pray for

Prayers for others

Answered prayers

DEPRESSION

Father God, I am not always sure why, but sometimes I feel depressed. I know that you provide love, peace, and joy. So, I know these feelings of depression don't come from you. Help me lean on You during these times and provide me with a trusted adult that I can talk with and get help. I ask these blessings in Jesus' name. Amen.

FOR I KNOW THE PLANS I HAVE FOR YOU," DECLARES THE LORD, "PLANS TO PROSPER YOU AND NOT TO HARM YOU, PLANS TO GIVE YOU HOPE AND A FUTURE.

Jeremiah 29:11

Today's verse

Date

Lord teach me

Lord guide me

Today I pray bor

Prayers for others

Answered prayers

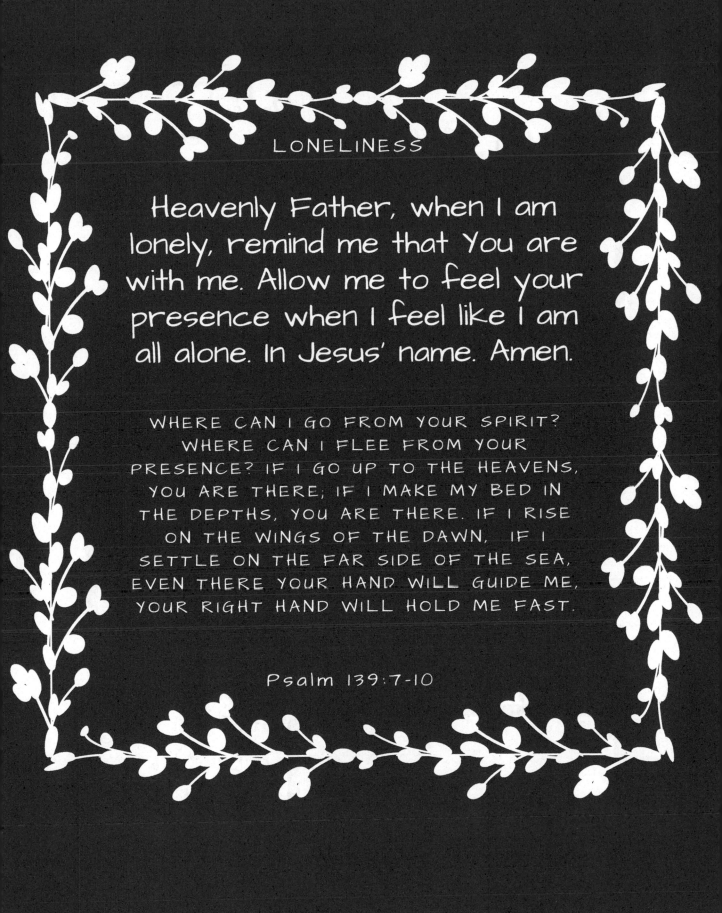

LONELINESS

Heavenly Father, when I am lonely, remind me that You are with me. Allow me to feel your presence when I feel like I am all alone. In Jesus' name. Amen.

WHERE CAN I GO FROM YOUR SPIRIT? WHERE CAN I FLEE FROM YOUR PRESENCE? IF I GO UP TO THE HEAVENS, YOU ARE THERE; IF I MAKE MY BED IN THE DEPTHS, YOU ARE THERE. IF I RISE ON THE WINGS OF THE DAWN, IF I SETTLE ON THE FAR SIDE OF THE SEA, EVEN THERE YOUR HAND WILL GUIDE ME, YOUR RIGHT HAND WILL HOLD ME FAST.

Psalm 139:7-10

Today's verse

Date

Lord teach me

Lord guide me

Today I pray for

Prayers for others

Answered prayers

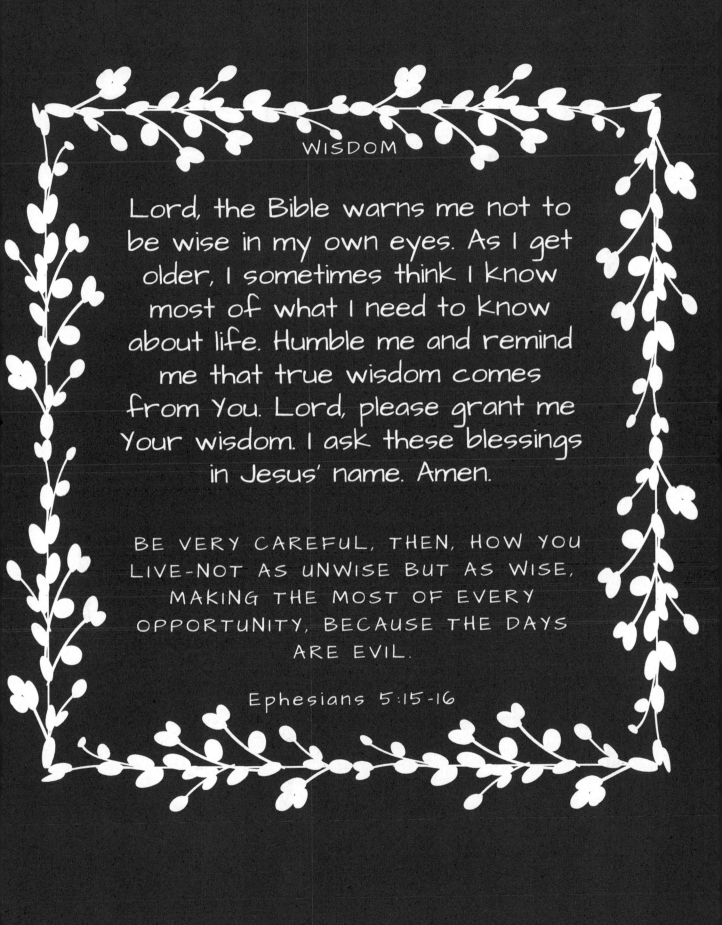

WISDOM

Lord, the Bible warns me not to be wise in my own eyes. As I get older, I sometimes think I know most of what I need to know about life. Humble me and remind me that true wisdom comes from You. Lord, please grant me Your wisdom. I ask these blessings in Jesus' name. Amen.

BE VERY CAREFUL, THEN, HOW YOU LIVE-NOT AS UNWISE BUT AS WISE, MAKING THE MOST OF EVERY OPPORTUNITY, BECAUSE THE DAYS ARE EVIL.

Ephesians 5:15-16

Today's verse

Date

Lord teach me

Lord guide me

Today I pray for

Prayers for others

Answered prayers

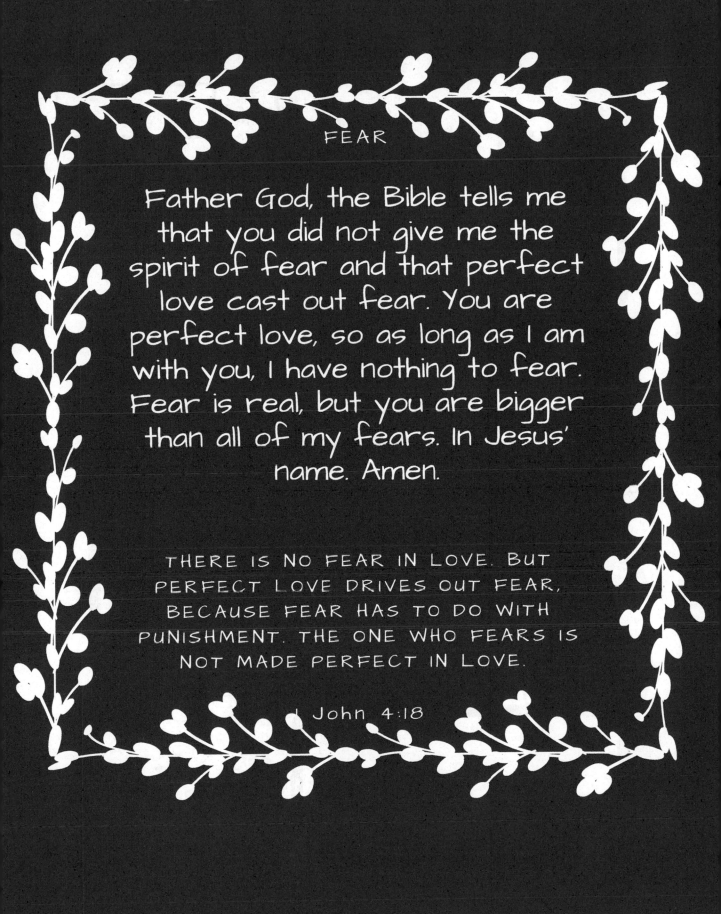

FEAR

Father God, the Bible tells me that you did not give me the spirit of fear and that perfect love cast out fear. You are perfect love, so as long as I am with you, I have nothing to fear. Fear is real, but you are bigger than all of my fears. In Jesus' name. Amen.

THERE IS NO FEAR IN LOVE. BUT PERFECT LOVE DRIVES OUT FEAR, BECAUSE FEAR HAS TO DO WITH PUNISHMENT. THE ONE WHO FEARS IS NOT MADE PERFECT IN LOVE.

1 John 4:18

Today's verse

Date

Lord teach me

Lord guide me

Today I pray for

Prayers for others

Answered prayers

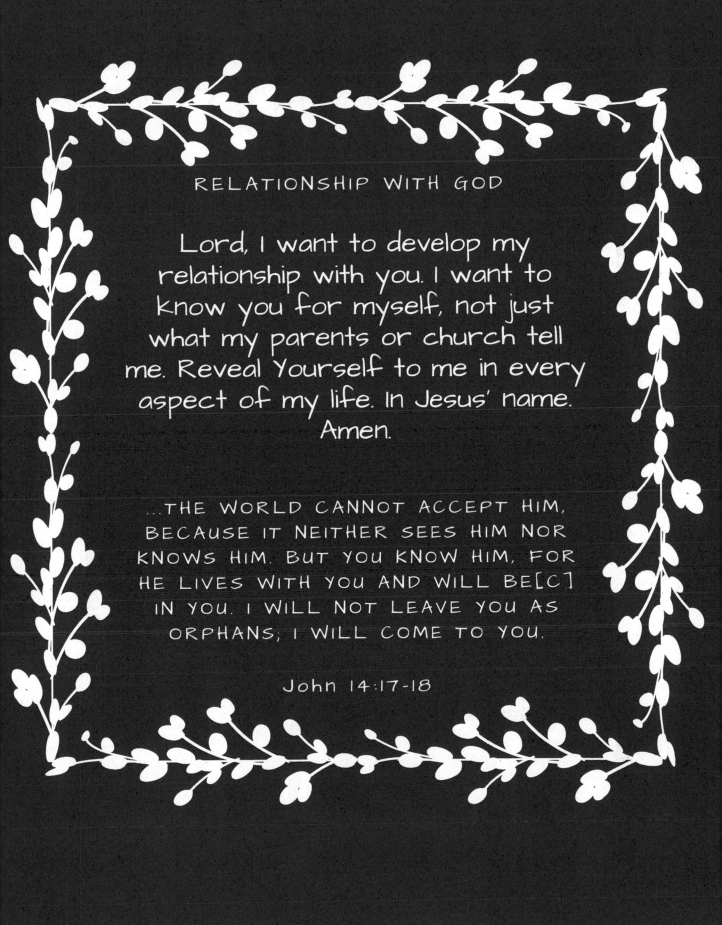

RELATIONSHIP WITH GOD

Lord, I want to develop my relationship with you. I want to know you for myself, not just what my parents or church tell me. Reveal Yourself to me in every aspect of my life. In Jesus' name. Amen.

...THE WORLD CANNOT ACCEPT HIM, BECAUSE IT NEITHER SEES HIM NOR KNOWS HIM. BUT YOU KNOW HIM, FOR HE LIVES WITH YOU AND WILL BE[C] IN YOU. I WILL NOT LEAVE YOU AS ORPHANS; I WILL COME TO YOU.

John 14:17-18

Today's verse

Date

Lord teach me

Lord guide me

Today I pray for

Prayers for others

Answered prayers

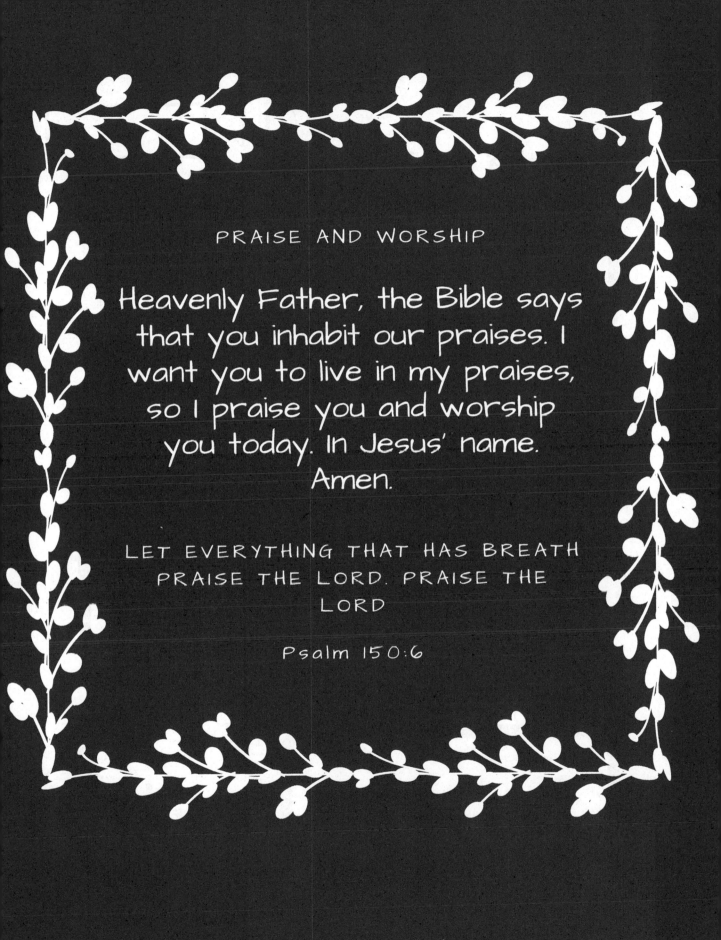

PRAISE AND WORSHIP

Heavenly Father, the Bible says that you inhabit our praises. I want you to live in my praises, so I praise you and worship you today. In Jesus' name. Amen.

LET EVERYTHING THAT HAS BREATH PRAISE THE LORD. PRAISE THE LORD

Psalm 150:6

Today I pray for

Prayers for others

Answered prayers

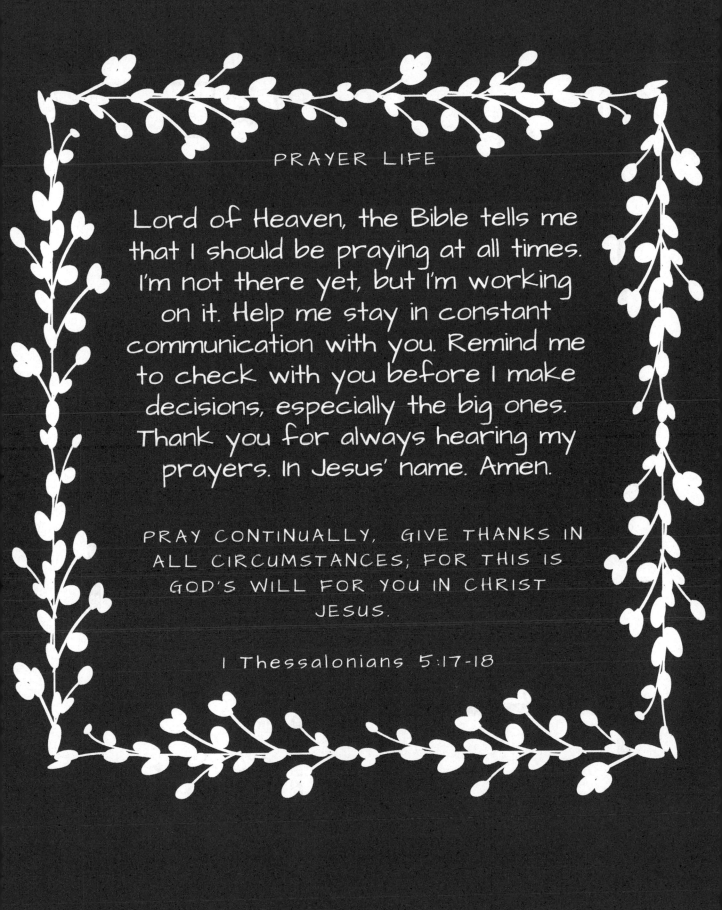

PRAYER LIFE

Lord of Heaven, the Bible tells me that I should be praying at all times. I'm not there yet, but I'm working on it. Help me stay in constant communication with you. Remind me to check with you before I make decisions, especially the big ones. Thank you for always hearing my prayers. In Jesus' name. Amen.

PRAY CONTINUALLY, GIVE THANKS IN ALL CIRCUMSTANCES; FOR THIS IS GOD'S WILL FOR YOU IN CHRIST JESUS.

1 Thessalonians 5:17-18

Today's verse

Date

Lord teach me

Lord guide me

Today I pray for

Prayers for others

Answered prayers

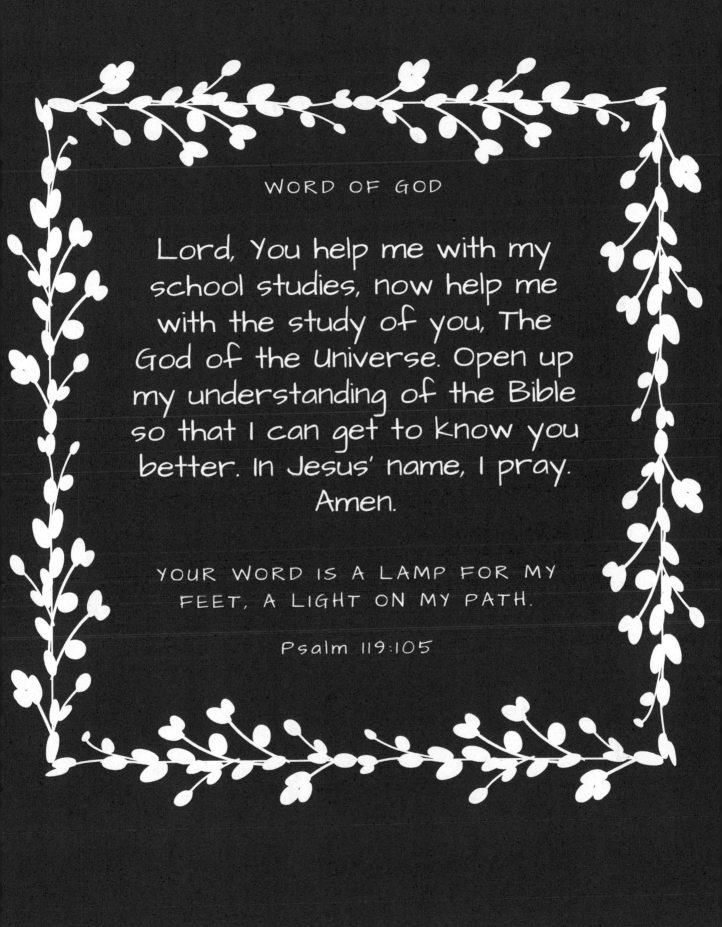

WORD OF GOD

Lord, You help me with my school studies, now help me with the study of you, The God of the Universe. Open up my understanding of the Bible so that I can get to know you better. In Jesus' name, I pray. Amen.

YOUR WORD IS A LAMP FOR MY FEET, A LIGHT ON MY PATH.

Psalm 119:105

Today's verse

Date

Lord teach me

Lord guide me

Today I pray for

Prayers for others

Answered prayers

HONORING GOD WITH YOUR LIFE

Lord of Heaven, show me how to honor you in all that I do, whether it be at school, church, volunteer opportunities, or work. When people see me, I want them to see You in me. In Jesus' name, I pray. Amen.

THEREFORE, I URGE YOU, BROTHERS AND SISTERS, IN VIEW OF GOD'S MERCY, TO OFFER YOUR BODIES AS A LIVING SACRIFICE, HOLY AND PLEASING TO GOD- THIS IS YOUR TRUE AND PROPER WORSHIP.

Romans 12:1

Today's verse

Date

Lord
teach me

Lord guide me

Today I pray for

Prayers for others

Answered prayers

HONORING YOUR MOTHER AND FATHER

Heavenly Father, allow me to honor my parents in all that I do. Remind me of all the wonderful things that they have instilled in me. Show me ways to give back to them. In Jesus' name, I pray. Amen.

HONOR YOUR FATHER AND YOUR MOTHER, SO THAT YOU MAY LIVE LONG IN THE LAND THE LORD YOUR GOD IS GIVING YOU.

Exodus 20:12

Today's verse

Date

Lord teach me

Lord guide me

Today I pray for

Prayers for others

Answered prayers

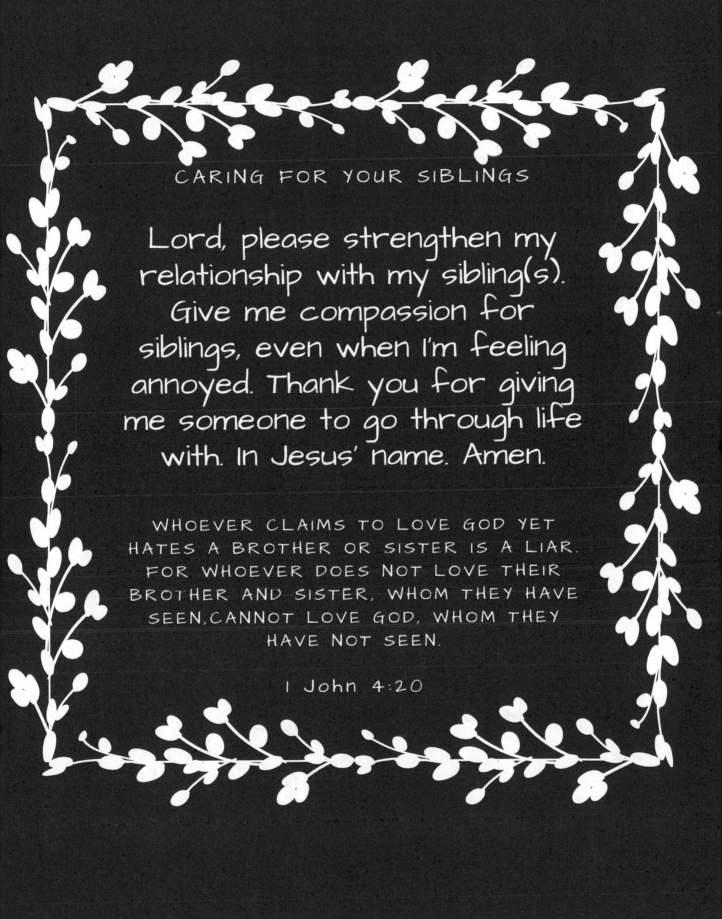

CARING FOR YOUR SIBLINGS

Lord, please strengthen my relationship with my sibling(s). Give me compassion for siblings, even when I'm feeling annoyed. Thank you for giving me someone to go through life with. In Jesus' name. Amen.

WHOEVER CLAIMS TO LOVE GOD YET HATES A BROTHER OR SISTER IS A LIAR. FOR WHOEVER DOES NOT LOVE THEIR BROTHER AND SISTER, WHOM THEY HAVE SEEN, CANNOT LOVE GOD, WHOM THEY HAVE NOT SEEN.

1 John 4:20

Today's verse

Date

Lord teach me

Lord guide me

Today I pray for

Prayers for others

Answered prayers

BEING HELPFUL IN YOUR HOME

Dear God, show me ways that I can be helpful in my home and contribute to my family. I am so blessed to have my family and home. Help me be a blessing in my home. In Jesus' name. Amen.

ANYONE WHO DOES NOT PROVIDE FOR THEIR RELATIVES, AND ESPECIALLY FOR THEIR OWN HOUSEHOLD, HAS DENIED THE FAITH AND IS WORSE THAN AN UNBELIEVER.

1 Timothy 5:8

Today's verse

Date

Lord teach me

Lord guide me

Today I pray for

Prayers for others

Answered prayers

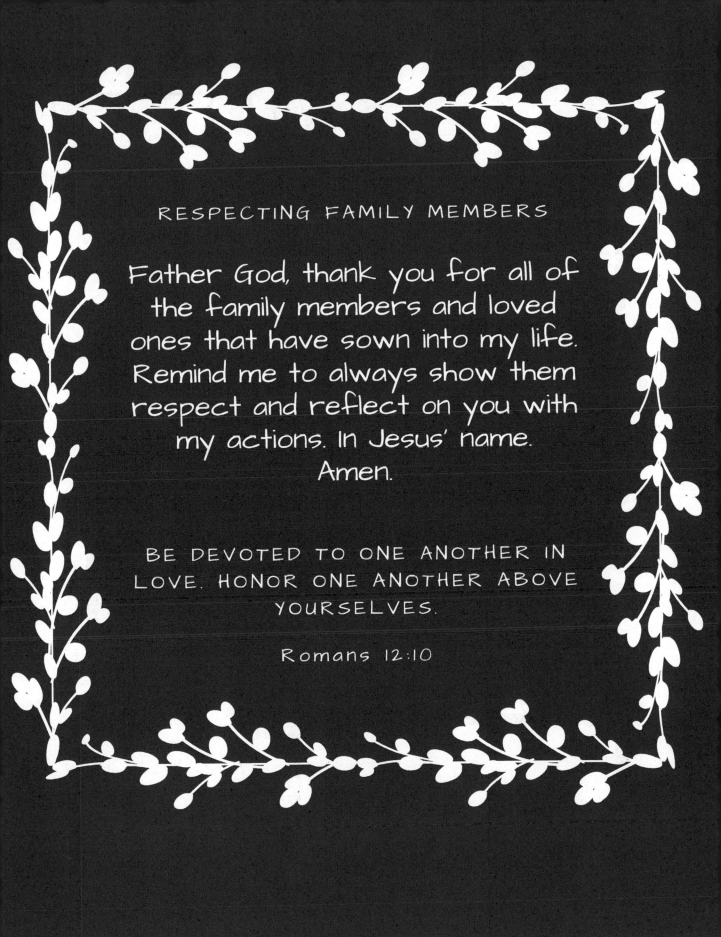

RESPECTING FAMILY MEMBERS

Father God, thank you for all of
the family members and loved
ones that have sown into my life.
Remind me to always show them
respect and reflect on you with
my actions. In Jesus' name.
Amen.

BE DEVOTED TO ONE ANOTHER IN
LOVE. HONOR ONE ANOTHER ABOVE
YOURSELVES.

Romans 12:10

Today's verse

Date

Lord teach me

Lord guide me

Today I pray for

Prayers for others

Answered prayers

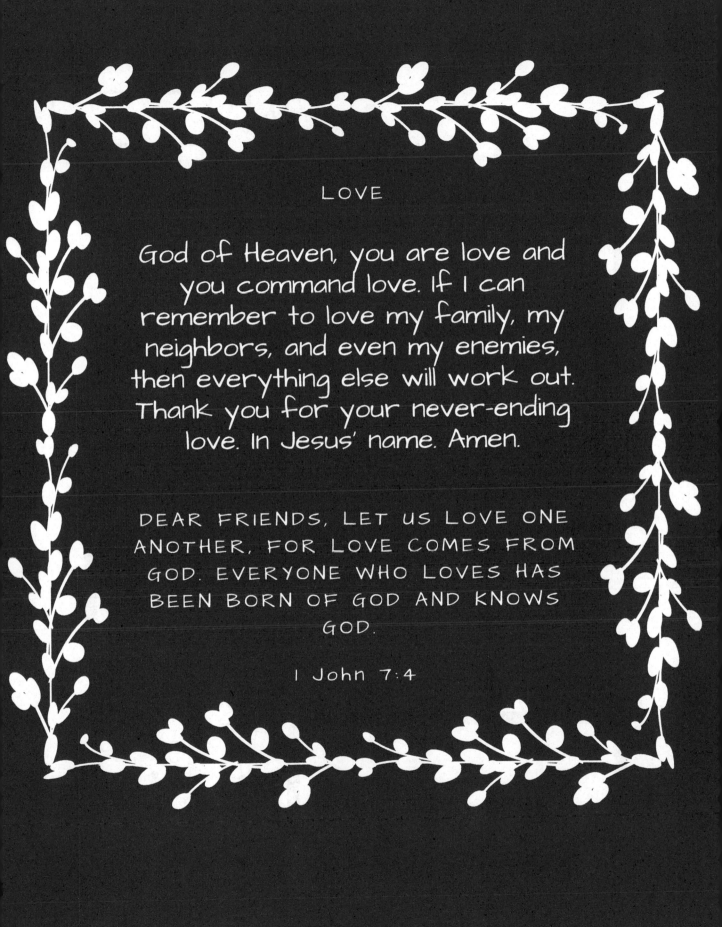

LOVE

God of Heaven, you are love and
you command love. If I can
remember to love my family, my
neighbors, and even my enemies,
then everything else will work out.
Thank you for your never-ending
love. In Jesus' name. Amen.

DEAR FRIENDS, LET US LOVE ONE
ANOTHER, FOR LOVE COMES FROM
GOD. EVERYONE WHO LOVES HAS
BEEN BORN OF GOD AND KNOWS
GOD.

1 John 7:4

Today's verse

Date

Lord teach me

Lord guide me

Today I pray for

Prayers for others

Answered prayers

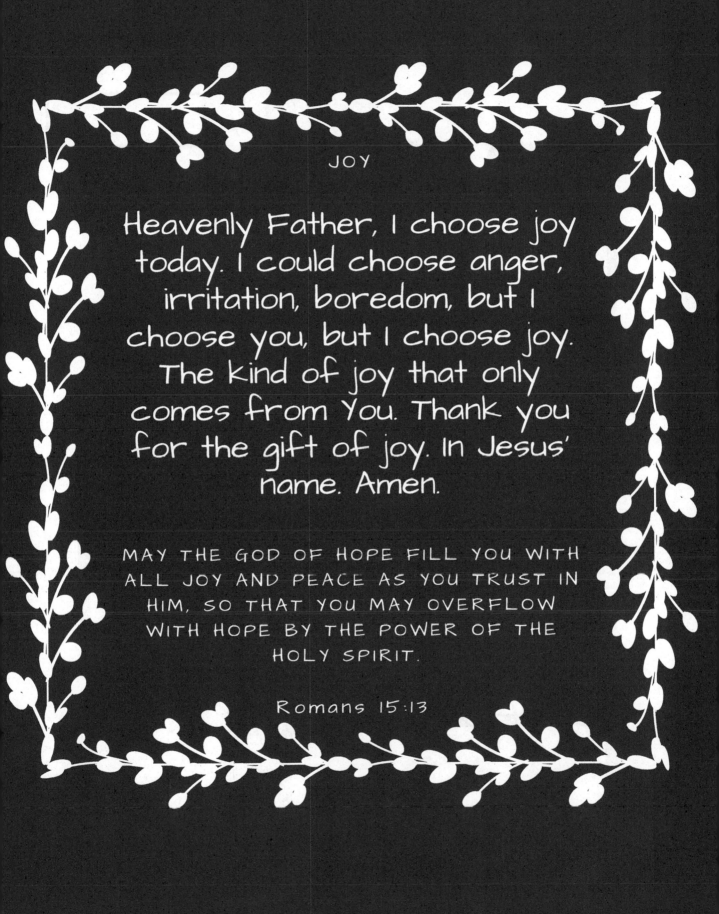

JOY

Heavenly Father, I choose joy today. I could choose anger, irritation, boredom, but I choose you, but I choose joy. The kind of joy that only comes from You. Thank you for the gift of joy. In Jesus' name. Amen.

MAY THE GOD OF HOPE FILL YOU WITH ALL JOY AND PEACE AS YOU TRUST IN HIM, SO THAT YOU MAY OVERFLOW WITH HOPE BY THE POWER OF THE HOLY SPIRIT.

Romans 15:13

Today's verse

Date

Lord teach me

Lord guide me

Today I pray for

Prayers for others

Answered prayers

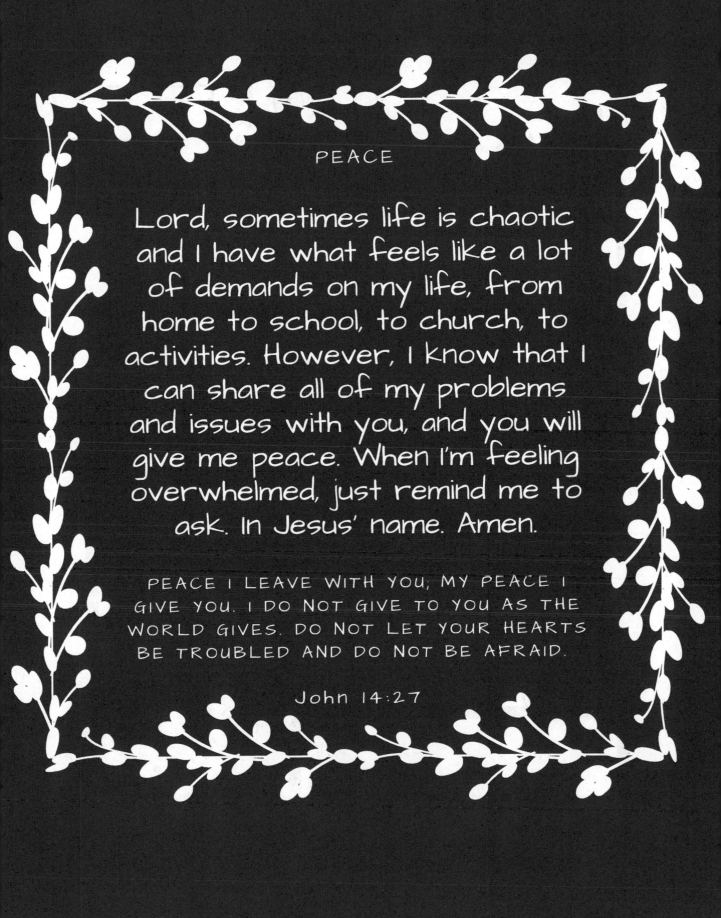

PEACE

Lord, sometimes life is chaotic and I have what feels like a lot of demands on my life, from home to school, to church, to activities. However, I know that I can share all of my problems and issues with you, and you will give me peace. When I'm feeling overwhelmed, just remind me to ask. In Jesus' name. Amen.

PEACE I LEAVE WITH YOU; MY PEACE I GIVE YOU. I DO NOT GIVE TO YOU AS THE WORLD GIVES. DO NOT LET YOUR HEARTS BE TROUBLED AND DO NOT BE AFRAID.

John 14:27

Today's verse

Date

Lord teach me

Lord guide me

Today I pray for

Prayers for others

Answered prayers

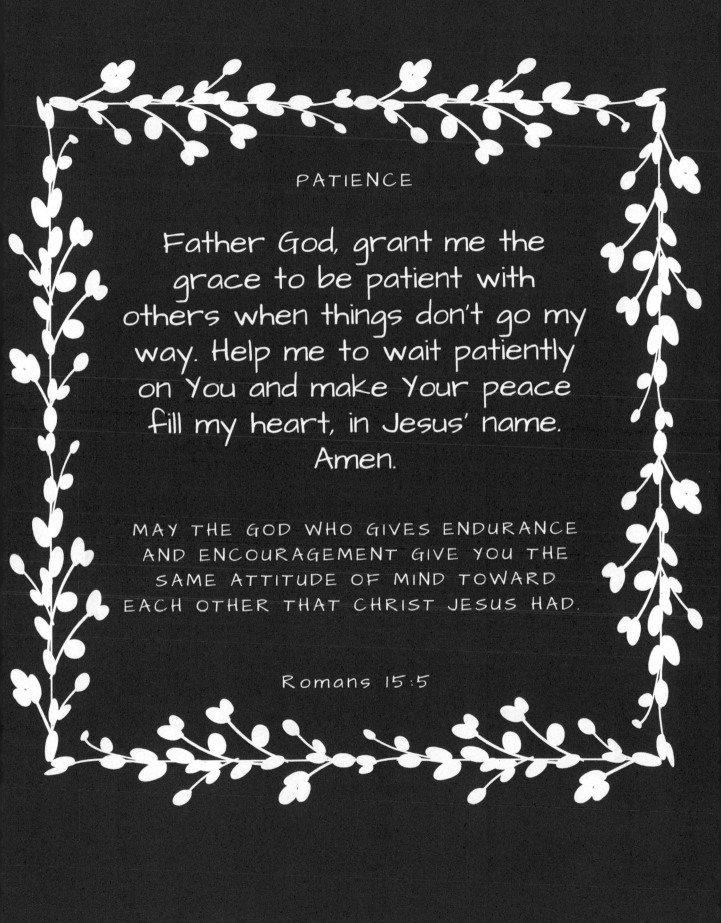

PATIENCE

Father God, grant me the grace to be patient with others when things don't go my way. Help me to wait patiently on You and make Your peace fill my heart, in Jesus' name. Amen.

MAY THE GOD WHO GIVES ENDURANCE AND ENCOURAGEMENT GIVE YOU THE SAME ATTITUDE OF MIND TOWARD EACH OTHER THAT CHRIST JESUS HAD.

Romans 15:5

Today's verse

Date

Lord teach me

Lord guide me

Today I pray for

Prayers for others

Answered prayers

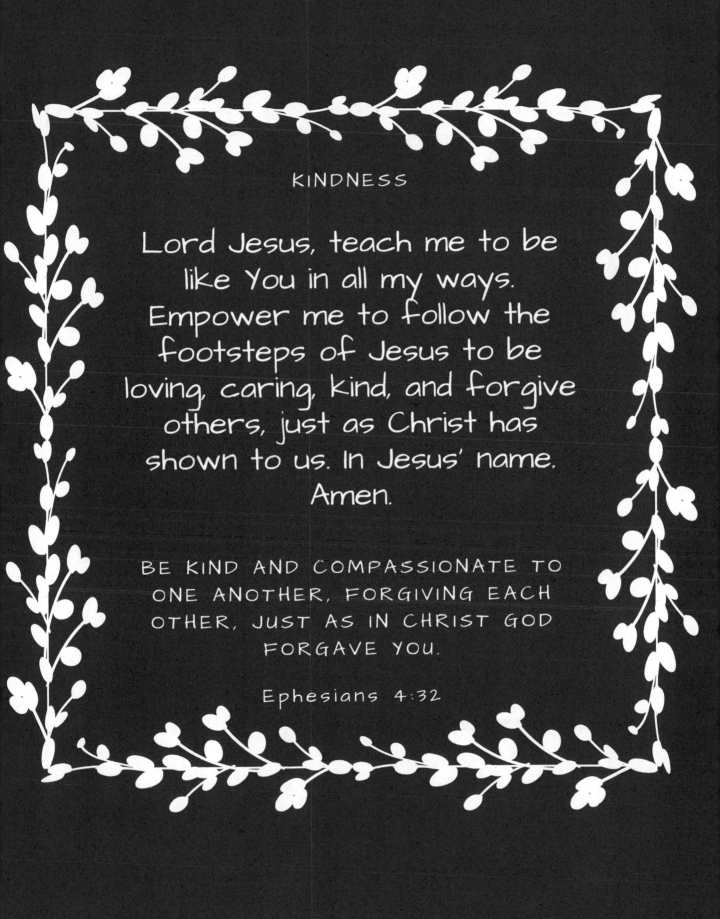

KINDNESS

Lord Jesus, teach me to be like You in all my ways. Empower me to follow the footsteps of Jesus to be loving, caring, kind, and forgive others, just as Christ has shown to us. In Jesus' name. Amen.

BE KIND AND COMPASSIONATE TO ONE ANOTHER, FORGIVING EACH OTHER, JUST AS IN CHRIST GOD FORGAVE YOU.

Ephesians 4:32

Today's verse

Date

Lord
teach me

Lord guide me

Today I pray for

Prayers for others

Answered prayers

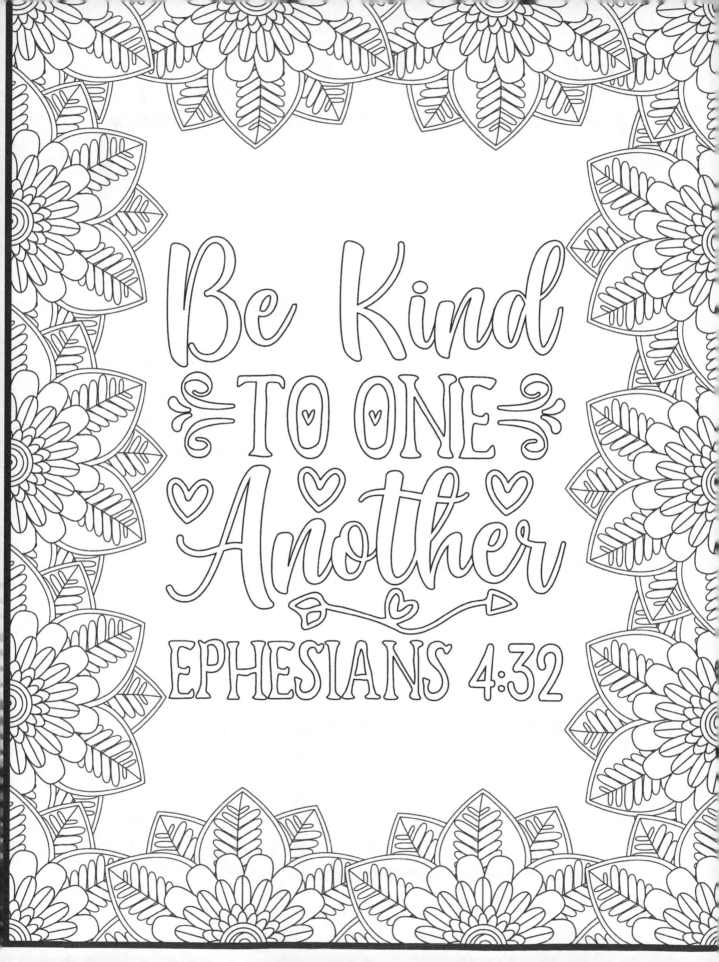

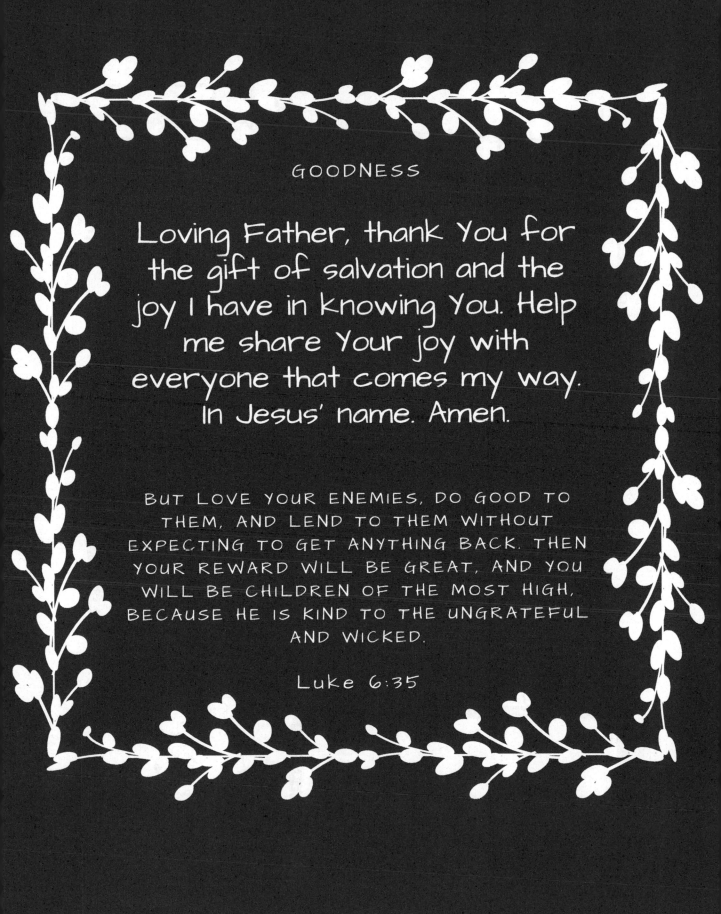

GOODNESS

Loving Father, thank You for the gift of salvation and the joy I have in knowing You. Help me share Your joy with everyone that comes my way. In Jesus' name. Amen.

BUT LOVE YOUR ENEMIES, DO GOOD TO THEM, AND LEND TO THEM WITHOUT EXPECTING TO GET ANYTHING BACK. THEN YOUR REWARD WILL BE GREAT, AND YOU WILL BE CHILDREN OF THE MOST HIGH, BECAUSE HE IS KIND TO THE UNGRATEFUL AND WICKED.

Luke 6:35

Today's verse

Date

Lord teach me

Lord guide me

Today I pray for

Prayers for others

Answered prayers

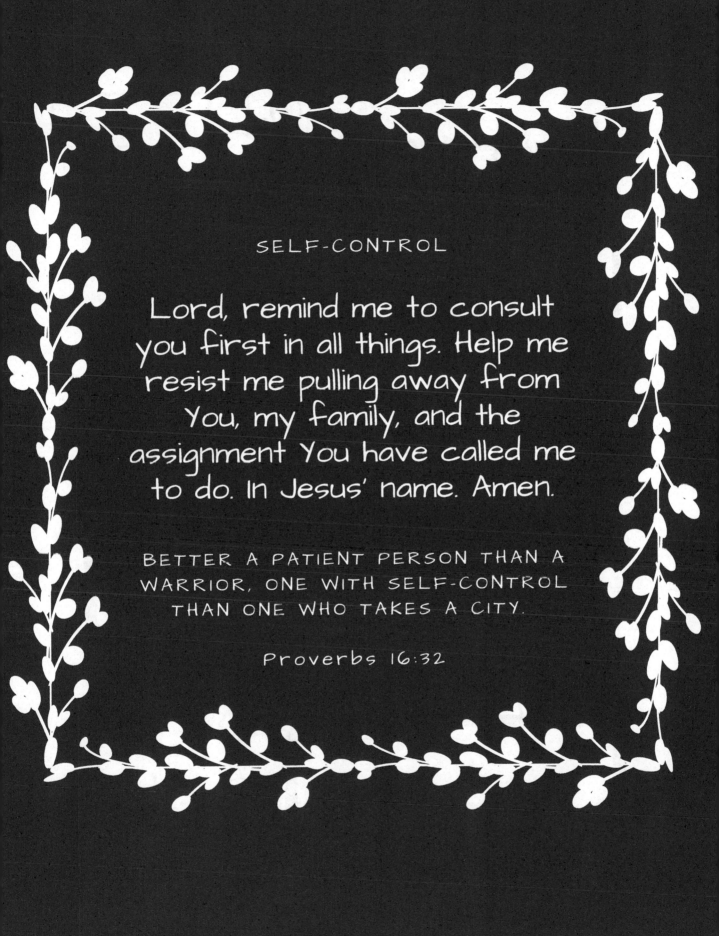

SELF-CONTROL

Lord, remind me to consult you first in all things. Help me resist me pulling away from You, my family, and the assignment You have called me to do. In Jesus' name. Amen.

BETTER A PATIENT PERSON THAN A WARRIOR, ONE WITH SELF-CONTROL THAN ONE WHO TAKES A CITY.

Proverbs 16:32

Today's verse

Date

Lord teach me

Lord guide me

Today I pray for

Prayers for others

Answered prayers

FAITHFULNESS

Heavenly Father, in the name of Jesus, help me to remain faithful to You and others, in truth and in action. Let every one of my actions show the character of Christ. Amen.

HIS MASTER REPLIED, 'WELL DONE, GOOD AND FAITHFUL SERVANT! YOU HAVE BEEN FAITHFUL WITH A FEW THINGS; I WILL PUT YOU IN CHARGE OF MANY THINGS. COME AND SHARE YOUR MASTER'S HAPPINESS!'

Matthew 25:21

Today's verse

Date

Lord
teach me

Lord guide me

Today I pray for

Prayers for others

Answered prayers

GENTLENESS

Father God, Take away every spirit of pride and arrogance from my life. Remind me to be gentle with all of your creations. Order my steps and direct my paths. In Jesus' name. Amen.

GRACIOUS WORDS ARE A HONEYCOMB, SWEET TO THE SOUL AND HEALING TO THE BONES.

Proverbs 16:24

Today's verse

Date

Lord teach me

Lord guide me

Today I pray for

Prayers for others

Answered prayers

Made in the USA
Columbia, SC
22 June 2023

18732186R00115